Contents

Sunderland College

Bede/Headways Learning Centre

This book is due for return on or before the last date shown below
Please be aware that sanctions are applied for overdue items
Renew online via Moodle
Renew by phone: call 5116344

1 3 FEB 2014		

Author __MARRIOTT, J__

Class __791·44__   Location Code __FM__

21 DAY LOAN

ALSO AVAILABLE IN THIS SERIES

Let the Right One In Anne Billson

Witchfinder General Ian Cooper

Saw Benjamin Poole

The Silence of the Lambs Barry Forshaw

The Texas Chain Saw Massacre James Rose

FORTHCOMING

Antichrist Amy Simmonds

The Blair Witch Project Peter Turner

Carrie Neil Mitchell

Halloween Murray Leeder

Nosferatu Christina Massaccesi

The Thing Jez Conolly

DEVIL'S ADVOCATES

THE DESCENT

JAMES MARRIOTT

Dedication

To my father, Richard Marriott, my first film-going companion.

Acknowledgements

Thanks to Jez Conolly, Kerri Sharp and John Atkinson at Auteur Publishing for getting this show on the road. Thanks also to draft readers for their useful feedback: John Coulthart, Adam Nevill, Dom Fripp, Matt Dunn.

First published in 2013 by
Auteur, 24 Hartwell Crescent, Leighton Buzzard LU7 1NP
www.auteur.co.uk
Copyright © Auteur 2013

Series design: Nikki Hamlett at Cassels Design
Set by Cassels Design www.casselsdesign.co.uk
Printed and bound by Short Run Press Ltd, Exeter, UK

British Library Cataloguing-in-Publication Data
A catalogue record for this book is available from the British Library

ISBN 978-1-906733-71-1

FOREWORD

STEPHEN THROWER

James Marriott's close reading of Neil Marshall's *The Descent* is a gem of accessible psychoanalytic film theory. Speaking as a reader of many texts on horror, it seems to me that psychoanalytical writing on the subject can often stray into aridity, dissertation-speak, convoluted argument and counter-argument and, worst of all, the dogmatic assertion of psychoanalysis as the primary index of truth. This book, however, is meticulous, open-minded and immensely readable. What distinguishes it is Marriott's clarity of engagement and his readiness to acknowledge branching points of view. There is no need to worry here about abstruse jargon, or the tendency – endemic for a while in psychoanalytic treatises on horror – to neglect the film under discussion in favour of plucking at some ingrown Freudian hair.

The enemy of plausibility in the discussion of cinema is reductionism; claims to final truth in film theory can alienate the reader as much as blizzards of jargon or discursive opacity. And yet, when discussing the meaning of what we see in the cinema, we inevitably wish to move from the specific to the general; 'it means whatever you want it to mean' is surely the least satisfying of attitudes. Moving from the discussion of a single character to that person as representative of their gender, social class, or some other ideological construction, takes the writer through a zone of contestation, one that not all negotiate with skill; the temptation can be to belabour the specifics with an ideological mallet until they turn into desirable generalities. Marriott draws upon feminist film theory, but stresses the inclusivity of his interpretations; a shared experience for men and women underpins the horror of *The Descent*, and Marriott does not allow his arguments to become encumbered with rhetorical banner-waving.

At the same time, since the film quite clearly intends for its female-only casting to be noticed, his engagement with feminist thinking on horror is pertinent and illuminating. Neither a soldier in the war against patriarchy, nor a blind adherent to social and sexual norms, he embraces the collective experience of trauma in the human animal and looks for heightened understanding through an engagement with cinema. Perhaps most importantly, he regards the obsessive compulsion to watch horror films (a strong component in fan behaviour) as a healing device that needs no deliverance through psychoanalysis. In a way, the fans are 'sisters doing it for themselves', dealing dynamically with their underlying problems through a willed and pleasurable return to unpleasure. James Marriott understood this, and he never lost sight of it in his writings on the horror genre, which always return to the love and excitement of film appreciation.

This is a concise and engaging book that demonstrates the continued relevance of the horror genre as a means to mitigate and comprehend the underlying pain of existence, a pain which leads back to the very earliest glimmerings of individual experience. I feel sure you will find it engrossing and thought-provoking. James Marriott's terribly premature death has robbed us of a passionate, clever and talented writer.

Stephen Thrower, March 2013

INTRODUCTION

By the end of the millennium it was easy to think that horror was a spent force. Japanese and other Asian spirit visitations provided some chilly kicks, but their parade of identikit long-haired wraiths, refugees from shampoo ads rather than scary or viscerally affecting films, quickly became tiresome, and lost even their faint shivers by the time of the inevitable American retreads.

By the middle of the '00s things looked different. British critic Alan Jones, writing for *Total Film* in 2006, coined the term the 'Splat Pack' to describe a group of directors – including Neil Marshall, Rob Zombie, Eli Roth and Darren Lynne Bousman – who were making films that were throwbacks, indeed often explicit homages, to a '70s US independent horror sensibility. The phrase caught on and the film industry paid attention: these movies were cheap to make and sold extremely well. But for all the critical ink spilled over the films' vaunted return to a '70s-styled political engagement, the most commercially successful of them – *Saw* (James Wan, 2004), *Hostel* (Eli Roth, 2005) – tended towards a dumb cartoonish posturing. The phrase 'torture porn', coined disapprovingly in 2006 by *New York Magazine* critic David Edelstein to describe the franchises launched by these films and their copycats, most accurately nails the films on their shabby scripts, lacklustre direction and a kind of witless hysteria that makes the viewer suspect that nobody – film-makers, viewers, critics – is meant to take these films seriously, effectively dismissing the radical potential of their '70s forebears.

Fortunately not all the films celebrated under the 'Splat Pack' rubric were so throwaway; some of the more intelligent, effective works even did well at the box office. To some viewers *The Descent* (Neil Marshall, 2005) marked a true return to form, providing a genuine version of what its peers could produce only as pastiche. For Mark Kermode, writing in the *Observer* (10 July 2005) it was 'one of the best British horror films of recent years'; Derek Elley in *Variety* (3 August 2006) described it as 'An object lesson in making a tightly-budgeted, no-star horror pic'; *Time Out*'s critic praised 'this fiercely entertaining British horror movie' (7 July 2005); and *Rolling Stone*'s Peter Travers (4 August 2006) warned prospective viewers to 'Prepare to be scared senseless'.

However favourable the response to the film, though, questions lingered in many viewers' minds. What exactly are the crawlers? (They remain unnamed in the film itself; the term comes from the end credits.) Are they a superfluous flourish in a film whose claustrophobic imagery of collapsing tunnels and snapping limbs is already horrific enough? Or does their presence push the film beyond the adventure/thriller genre into the domain of horror proper? How much do the events depicted in the film happen in its diegetic reality, and how much are they a projection of Sarah's mind? What difference does it make that this is an all-female group of cavers?

In this book I'll attempt to answer these and other questions. The Descent can, of course, be enjoyed 'straight', as a purely visceral thrill-ride, but it also invites other, more speculative readings.

The book is structured as follows:

The Descent is a detailed synopsis of the film. This serves to clarify what actually happens (going by the reviews the film has been for certain viewers a confusing experience) and to introduce some speculative ideas that don't fit neatly anywhere else. If you've just watched the film you may want to skip this section for now.

The Shock of the Old explores the lure of atavism in horror, and suggests where The Descent might fit in to this tradition.

Going Underground looks at caves in and out of horror films, and asks which of several millennia-worth of cave associations are mobilised in The Descent.

One Million Years BC wonders what exactly the crawlers are, and compares them to cannibalistic cave-dwellers in everything from The Mole People (Virgil V. Vogel, 1956) to Ravenous (Antonia Bird, 1999).

Return to the Source analyses the womb imagery permeating the film, and asks what's so scary about being born.

Chicks with Picks wonders what difference it makes that Marshall's party is women only, and investigates The Descent's contribution to the thorny issue of the representation of women in horror films.

Nightmares in a Damaged Brain examines Sarah's mental health and finds it distinctly lacking, leading to a discussion of why mad women are different from mad men in the movies.

Family works out which films Neil Marshall was watching while he wrote *The Descent*, sits through lots of films set in caves so that you don't have to, and then casts a sunlight-starved eye over the rash of cave films that followed *The Descent*'s release.

Conclusion rounds up the principle theories applied to the reading of the film, placing them in the context of the genre's efficacy at addressing the compulsion to control and manage trauma.

Detailed analyses of films contain spoilers, I'm afraid; it's not always possible to discuss a film without mentioning what actually happens in it. A certain amount of familiarity is assumed with the horror classics Marshall references in *The Descent*; if you haven't seen *Deliverance* (John Boorman, 1972), *Alien* (Ridley Scott, 1979), *The Shining* (Stanley Kubrick, 1980) or *The Thing* (John Carpenter, 1982) yet, you should put this book down and rent the DVDs.

Occasionally a film's original release title isn't the title by which it is most widely known. When a film is first mentioned it'll have full details – original and English language / alternate title, director and year of release – listed; in subsequent references it'll just have the title by which it's best known. So *WIthIN* (Olatunde Osunsanmi, 2005) becomes *The Cavern* and *Alien 2 – Sulla terra* (Ciro Ippolito, 1980) becomes *Alien Terror*.

INTRODUCING NEIL MARSHALL

Marshall was born in Newcastle upon Tyne in England in 1970. Inspired by an early viewing of *Raiders of the Lost Ark* (Steven Spielberg, 1981) he made Super 8 home movies and went to film school at Newcastle Polytechnic (now Northumbria University). He cut his industry teeth as a freelance editor before being hired in 1995 to co-write and edit *Killing Time* (Bharat Nalluri, 1998).

As a writer-director with four films in a decade under his belt – *Dog Soldiers* (2002), *The Descent, Doomsday* (2008) and *Centurion* (2010) (two of which, *Dog Soldiers* and *Doomsday*, he also edited) – Marshall has some claim to auteur status, and indeed there are several key themes to which the director has returned throughout his career. All of his films to date have been either set or shot, at least partially, in Scotland. Marshall is English, but clearly has an affinity for the Scots; his hometown of Newcastle is historically situated on Hadrian's Wall, the Roman border recreated in *Doomsday* and alluded to in *Centurion*, so he may feel an ancestral kinship.

Marshall sidesteps many of the problems associated with the cinema of 'small nations' like Scotland by making genre films, for which the landscape is well suited, rather than celebrations of a heritage landscape and the myth-making that attends them (*Braveheart* [Mel Gibson, 1995] or *Rob Roy* [Michael Caton-Jones, 1995]) or kitchen-sink dramas like *Neds* (Peter Mullen, 2010).

There is a kind of celebration of the landscape in Marshall's films – Scotland looks spectacular – but it is characteristically depicted as hostile, shot in a cold blue light, filled with midges and ticks and an unforgiving drizzle that means Marshall won't be called on to shoot a campaign for Visit Scotland any time soon. While none of his films is overtly 'about' Scotland, a patchwork image of the country and a subtle politics emerges over their course: the Scots are a feisty, no bullshit people, given to resisting control (both in *Centurion*'s past and *Doomsday*'s future) but condemned to be mistreated by a colonising power, used as little more than a petri dish for experiments on either a small (*Dog Soldiers*) or large (*Doomsday*) scale.

Marshall's affinity for the Scots has its roots in a general sympathy for the underdog. The werewolves of *Dog Soldiers* are the result of a military experiment they are guaranteed not to have signed up for; the crawlers of *The Descent* are simply protecting their territory and looking for lunch; the feral characters of *Doomsday* have been abandoned to their fate by a heartless and distant English government; and the Picts of *Centurion* have suffered terribly at the hands of the Romans. Feral is a key term here: Marshall's underdogs are wild, to the extent of being either part-animal (*Dog Soldiers*, *The Descent*), dressing in skins (*Centurion*) or demonstrating table manners that just won't cut it in polite society (*Doomsday*).

Although Marshall has made two outright horror films, and uses horror imagery in his other films, he has a strictly materialist worldview with no room for the supernatural. The werewolves in *Dog Soldiers* are creations of science, and *The Descent* sidesteps any real consideration of its caves as entrances to hell, or the underworld, and instead pushes any surplus weirdness it may have into the realms of psychology. The Scots of *Doomsday* may have regressed, but not to the point where they believe in magic; and while the female characters in *Centurion* are believed by some to have magical powers – Etain's tracking ability and Aeron's (Axelle Carolyn) witchy isolation – the film is careful to reject these ideas as groundless superstition.

Marshall has an enthusiasm and a gift for action sequences, which is easily exploited in answering the basic question posed by his films: what happens to a group of professionals when they encounter something unexpected? If his films can be generically united at all it is under an 'action-adventure' rubric. This comes with its own macho pitfalls, which Marshall avoids up to a point by replacing chest-beating leaders with more engagingly self-doubting characters in *Dog Soldiers* and *Centurion*, and by filling his films with tough female characters. Unfortunately these characters only tend to be tough insofar as they behave like men; Aeron in *Centurion* marks a welcome change in Marshall's depiction of women, being both strong and feminine. Aeron is also one of the few trustworthy women in Marshall's films; as explored elsewhere (see **Chicks with Picks**), Cooper's assertion in *Dog Soldiers* that he fears 'spiders ... women. Spider women' would seem to fit fairly neatly on to any of Marshall's films.

Marshall's focus on the dynamics of leadership betrays a broader concern with the needs of the individual versus the needs of the group. In each of his films a group is pitted against an enemy; in *Centurion* most of the group are strangers and potential enemies to each other. Marshall's love of war films is evident in his films' conviction that the group is paramount. Maverick loners, far from being celebrated, as they might be in, say, the rugged individualism of a Don Siegel film, are characteristically portrayed as sly and untrustworthy.

Marshall is more comfortable showing a gory eye injury than people having sex; indeed there are no sex scenes in his films. Perhaps he feels, like Ridley Scott (an obvious influence), that sex is boring unless you are doing it yourself.

Finally, he is obviously highly cine-literate, and is happy to quote from other films; thankfully this never becomes tiresome, as in some Tarantino films, and Marshall never makes simple collages of scenes from other films (although *Doomsday* comes close) but rather keeps his own idiosyncratic flavour throughout.

APPROACHING *THE DESCENT*

Although Marshall was happy with the tone of his first feature, the 'werewolves ate my platoon' picture *Dog Soldiers*, he realised that it was less a full-on horror film than 'a black comedy with some horror elements in it. It kind of went over the top' (in Stax, 2006). After seeing video footage of a cave-diving expedition he began work on a script called 'The Dark', with a view to making a truly scary film, and a tribute to the '70s classics of horror cinema: 'I wanted [the film] to be hard-hitting and back-to-basics brutal because it was the '70s-styled survival picture I've always wanted to make' (in Jones 103-4).

The idea was pitched to Christian Colson of Celador Films, and the two spent the following two years and eight drafts developing the script, until Marshall was happy with the credibility of the characters. Celador provided about £5 million in financing and casting focused on using relatively unknown actresses who would be able to withstand the physical demands of the shoot. Exterior shooting commenced in Scotland in December 2004 and the production then moved to Pinewood to shoot the sequences in the cave, built and inventively recycled on studio soundstages.

The film's US distributor, Lionsgate, responded to strong word of mouth by securing US distribution rights two weeks before the film opened in the UK in July 2005. The film had a moderately successful theatrical run in the UK, earning around £3.5 million, and similar sums in other European territories. Lionsgate delayed the US theatrical release until August 2006, to avoid confusion with rival caving film *The Cave* (Bruce Hunt, 2005), and trimmed the ending of the film so that it finished with Sarah seeing Juno sitting beside her in the SUV. According to Marshall he had considered ending the film at this point himself as he was frustrated during the film's rushed post-production, although he was eventually able to complete it according to his original script. Lionsgate found the trimmed ending tested better with US audiences than the original ending, but needed

Marshall's permission to cut. Marshall agreed to this edit on the understanding that the film would get a wide theatrical release. The film went on to make $26 million during its ten-week US theatrical run.

That Marshall has described his original ending as being inspired by *Brazil* (Terry Gilliam, 1985) – 'what is a true happy ending? If that character in their own mind is happy, then is that a happy ending regardless of their physical circumstances?' (in Valdez, 2008) – is ironic given Gilliam's noted battle to have his film released in the US intact. Marshall's pragmatism may rest ultimately on the knowledge that theatrical runs are perhaps not even half the story nowadays, and Lionsgate duly released an 'uncut' DVD of the film with its original ending intact. For the purposes of this book, the film is considered in its entirety, i.e. with the original ending.

THE DESCENT

The film opens with a shot of pine forest and clouds. The light is cold, the day beginning to darken. We see three women white-water rafting in a succession of rapid edits. Two, who turn out to be Sarah (Shauna Macdonald) and Beth (Alex Reid), are wearing blue; Juno (Natalie Mendoza), the third, is wearing pink. Juno is on one side of the raft, the others opposite her. A man and a young girl, who also wears blue, wave to them. Immediately several themes are established. The white-water rafting looks risky, dangerous; the river is clearly a hostile environment and there is a pervasive sense of cold. We are reminded of *Deliverance*, more adventure tourism on an unforgiving river. Juno is marked off from the rest of the group – the rest of the women, if we include the girl – not only by her position on the raft but also the colour of her clothes; we might note that her pink is a colour traditionally coded as feminine, while the other women's clothes are blue, traditionally coded as masculine. Whether we take conscious stock of this or not, this is clearly a group of women indulging in extreme sports while one of their husbands looks after their daughter, a reversal, perhaps, of traditional gender roles.

When they have passed their final set of rapids the women's roles become clearer: Sarah waves at the man and child, marking her as wife and mother; Juno is pushed into the water by Beth, again marking her as slightly apart, separate. While Sarah makes directly for her daughter Jessica (Molly Kayll) her husband Paul (Oliver Milburn) helps to pull Juno out of the water, and even takes off her helmet. Beth, tying up the dinghy, notices the intimacy of the exchange and frowns. Paul, aware that Beth has noticed, tells Jessica to come back to the car as it's freezing, reinforcing our sense of the cold. Sarah offers to help with the dinghy but Beth, perhaps attempting to encourage a closer relationship between Sarah and her husband, tells her to join Paul and Jessica. Sarah has a marked Scottish accent; Beth and Paul seem to be English, and when we hear Juno speak, which is not until later, she appears to be American. The scene provides us with subtle information about the group dynamic: Sarah's principal familial relationship is with Jessica rather than Paul; Paul and Juno share a closeness, probably inappropriate given how quickly Paul turns away when he notices Beth watching; Beth disapproves of this intimacy and is keen for Sarah to protect her marriage.

Cut to the interior of a car. Sarah is chatting with Jessica, then touches Paul, who flinches from her touch. She asks him if he's OK, he seems a bit distant. He turns to tell her he's fine, as through the windscreen we watch a van heading towards them. The crash is shown initially from inside the car, then from the side; piping from the roof of the van flies through the air and the windscreen, and we are shown its effect by a shot of the back of Paul's headrest as one of the pipes skewers his skull. The camera pans up and away from the wreckage of the van and car, suggesting perhaps a release of spirits, rising from the site of the accident. Fade to black.

The accident raises several questions. Why introduce characters, only to kill them off so early – at 3 minutes 40 seconds – in the film? Is Sarah responsible for the accident by distracting her husband? Could anyone have survived such an accident?

This last question seems to be answered when the film fades in on the image of a birthday cake, lit by the five candles arranged on its top, the words 'Happy birthday Jessica' legible although they are upside down to the viewer. Cut to a shot of a very damaged-looking Sarah in a hospital bed as she awakens. Becoming aware of where she is, she pulls various sensors off her arms, making her heart monitor flatline, and walks out into the corridor.

The name on her lips is 'Jess', reinforcing our sense that she is far closer to her daughter than to her husband; perhaps she suspects, or knows, that he has betrayed her (although nowhere in the film do we learn definitively the extent of Juno's relationship with Paul); or, conversely, perhaps he has sought companionship elsewhere because her closeness to her daughter has left no room for him. The lights go off behind her, in a well-defined block with a sound effect of something shutting down. The remaining light has a crisp edge clearly demarcating it from the darkness beyond; this is not how light behaves, marking the scene as a hallucination or fantasy. More lights go off and we watch Sarah's face while the corridor recedes behind her in a dizzying *Jaws*-style dolly counter zoom. She races down the corridor towards the small remaining patch of light at the end, seemingly chased by the darkness, until we cut to an image of her in a well-lit hospital corridor, evidently in the 'real' world, screaming 'Jessie!' as she crouches on the floor in the arms of Beth. Juno is behind them, unnoticed. As Sarah weeps Juno too begins to cry, turns before the others see her and flees.

It's only now that the title of the film is shown, appearing as though a torch were playing over the letters; the typeface is one familiar to film buffs as that used by John Carpenter in many of his 1980s films. Another shot of forests follows, backed by a darkening sky, marked on-screen as 'Appalachian Mountains, USA' although it looks similar to the forest shots that open the film – and was, indeed, again shot in Scotland. The Appalachian reference again raises the spectre of *Deliverance* and any number of the 'urbanoia' films (the term is Carol Clover's and refers to the violent 'city vs country' film inspired by Boorman's model) that followed in its wake, while the aerial shot of a car speeding through the forest recalls the opening of *The Shining*.

The title sequence introduces David Julyan's principal music score for the film – an instantly memorable sequence of string chords ascending and descending, which avoids horror clichés, and would fit equally well in an endurance film such as *Touching the Void* (Kevin Macdonald, 2003), with its epic, stirring feel. Critical opinion has been divided over the score: where Marshall was reportedly delighted, some critics have complained that it is overly bombastic or even 'harrumphing', to use Mark Kermode's memorable term. It is one year on from the accident. Beth is driving a distinctly haunted-looking Sarah to what we soon understand to be some kind of reunion. The *Deliverance* references mount: Beth spins the radio dial but can only find bluegrass and religious channels, and suggests to Sarah that they bail on their plan, get wasted and go to a barn dance. Her tone is dismissive, jokey, reminding us of the city–country insults and arrogance that always precede hillbilly vengeance in films of the *Deliverance* model. The point is reinforced when they drive past a sign, pockmarked with shotgun holes, welcoming them to 'Chatooga National Park'. The Chatooga is the name of the river that gets Lewis and the boys in trouble in *Deliverance*, and even if we don't get the reference, the shot marks remind us that this is an area where gun ownership is the norm, the locals probably won't take kindly to outsiders, and mental defectives with plaid shirts and rotting teeth are probably operating a moonshine still just around the corner. All of this, of course, is a deliberate red herring: *The Descent* may share many qualities with *Deliverance*, but homicidal hillbillies is not one of them.

Beth's barn dance suggestion is intended to let Sarah know that she can still back out of the plan; Sarah acknowledges this but tells Beth she doesn't want to be the one to tell

Juno. Again Juno is marked as separate from the others, not only the group leader but also authoritarian, somebody the others like to grouch about.

Marshall throws in another red herring as Beth and Sarah arrive at a log cabin in the woods. Actually found for the shoot in some woods not far from London, the setting recalls any number of horror films where something nasty happens in the forest, perhaps most strongly *The Evil Dead* (Sam Raimi, 1981). As with the Scottish scenes opening the film, the light here has a bluish cast and the women are wearing jumpers: it's clearly cold.

Sarah is welcomed into the house by Juno. She knows Sam (MyAnna Buring) and Rebecca (Saskia Mulder) already: they are sisters whose nationality is unclear (I believe they are meant to be Swedish), with Sam given one of the characters' few explicit occupations in being a medical student. Sarah thanks Sam for a letter but goes no further than this in referring to the past; it's clear that the women are treading on eggshells in trying to reintegrate Sarah into their community. Implicit in this is the assumption that Sarah has not seen any of them (apart from Beth, marked from the outset as her closest friend) since her accident; indeed, that she hasn't really been doing much at all since the accident. The others are careful to avoid any reference to the accident in talking to Sarah, a development that's realistic enough although it's not clear that this is what she actually wants or needs.

The women's ages are slightly unclear. Sam tells Beth 'I hear it all starts falling apart at twenty-five', and Beth's later comment – 'Could anyone make me feel any older?' – suggests that she is the oldest in the group. This may also account for her slight hostility towards Holly (Nora-Jane Noone), her 'here we go' aside as Juno's 'protégé' and perhaps the youngest of the group enters the room. Holly – a base-jumping enthusiast who moved to the US when she 'ran out of things to jump off in Galway', clearly more motivated by the adrenalin rush than the others – responds in kind with 'You must be the teacher', ie: you look like the oldest in the group.

Some viewers have complained about the scene that follows: the women drink beer and reminisce in what has struck some as a pointless scene-setting exercise, and one that moreover fails in its evident aim of introducing the women and allowing us to differentiate between them. I would disagree. The scene is important in establishing various subtle fault lines in the group dynamic, while the differentiation seems fairly realistic: rather than opting for unrealistically distinct character types, Marshall presents a group whose credibility is actually enhanced by an apparent initial similarity, as though the viewer has been introduced around at a party or a new workplace and has trouble remembering exactly who everyone is. This credibility, along with the length of the scene, demonstrates that the film has a certain compassion for its characters, prompting a copycat response from the viewer. These characters are neither ciphers nor witless irritants, and the film spends some time building them up as credible individuals.

Holly's discussion of her own adrenalin adventures prompts reminiscences from the others about their climbing days, as they all crowd around a photo Juno pulls out. This suggests that the group used to meet up more regularly, and introduces a note of tension relating to the women's ages, which the film picks up more strongly later on. It also prompts Sarah to say 'Love each day', and to explain that it was something Paul used to say. The camera focuses on Juno's response, indicating again an implicit relationship between Juno and Sarah's husband, and Sarah's comment casts a pall over the evening as the others fall silent. It is left to Sarah herself to rescue the atmosphere, which she does with an invitation to drink.

Holly and Sam go outside to smoke a joint. Holly slates Boreham Caverns, their planned destination, as a tourist trap: 'might as well have guard rails and a fucking giftshop'. This is the first indication, the title aside, that the women plan to visit a cave. They try to hide the joint when Juno comes out, evidently keen not to upset the boss; Juno fingers a pendant around her neck as she tells them tomorrow will be 'awesome'.

Fade in on the tops of empty beer bottles; the evening is obviously well advanced and the discussion has turned to relationships. Sam talks about her boyfriend, and Holly, answering Sarah's question about whether or not she has a partner, describes herself as a 'sports fuck' like Juno and Rebecca, but tells them that she wants to have lots of babies when she's older. The camera is on Sarah at this point, who seems discomfited; and this awkwardness provides a natural break to end the scene.

Cut to Sarah in bed. It is still night, but we can see by a bluish, lunar light. There is a bottle of pills, out of focus but clearly present, by the side of her bed. She is sharing a room with Beth. She gets up, fully clothed, and goes to the window. As she peers out a pipe suddenly shoots through the window and into her eye socket, prompting her to wake up from the dream. Unlike the earlier hallucination or fantasy sequence in the hospital, this is shot exactly like the surrounding footage, casting some doubt on the trustworthiness of the subsequent events. This sequence features a set of near-subliminal sound cues, suggesting that Sarah's story might not be entirely stable. Just before the pole crashes through the window, there is a faint, time-stretched sound that anticipates the crawlers' echolocating clicks.

Juno is, of course, the first up, and is seen running in the dawn light before waking the others up. Rebecca screams in the shower, and the film cuts Hitchcock-style to Beth screaming into a mirror. Sarah takes some pills then leaves the bottle behind, presumably expecting to be back later that day. The others argue over who will drive each of their 4WDs to the cave until Sarah volunteers, clearly willing to get involved. An automatic photo is taken of the group, which we see in a black and white freeze frame.

The group travels towards the cave in two vehicles, again recalling *Deliverance*. Sarah drives fast, recklessly, and Beth warns her to slow down; Sarah's riposte is that she's having fun, and Juno repeats this approvingly. In the other car Rebecca, Sam and Holly discuss the cave: none of them has been there before, but Rebecca assures Sam that it's 'quite safe' as it's Level 2. Too safe for Holly, who describes it as 'Boredom Caves'.

Juno deliberately leaves the guidebook in the car, an obvious harbinger of doom, although not perhaps quite for the reasons we expect. The group walks up through forest towards the cave. Rebecca demonstrates her safety-first attitude and not incidentally gives the viewer a primer on caving protocol: 'Rule number 1: file a flight plan and stick to it. Rule number 2: don't go wandering off. When you think it's dark when you turn out the light, well down there it's pitch black. You can get dehydration, disorientation, claustrophobia' – we hear a 'yeah, yeah, yeah' from one of the others, who has clearly heard all this before – 'panic attacks, paranoia, hallucinations, visual and aural …' Her voice peters out, drowned out by the score and the group walking away from the camera. If Sarah's two hallucination/dreams so far have not been enough of an indication, this makes it explicit: some of what we see subsequently may well be a hallucination.

They find the corpse of an elk. Holly takes a photo, marking her as a near-obsessive recorder of events, a theme picked up on later. They speculate casually about what might have killed the elk; Juno says that it 'Could have been Bigfoot for all you know' in a bid to get them moving. This marks another red herring concerning the dangers they may face, or at least a partial red herring: the crawlers are relict hominids, after all, but more human than the broadly ape-like Bigfoot. If the crawlers have killed the elk, the question of why they have left its carcass in the open air rather than dragging it into the cave is unanswered.

Juno leads them further up alongside a stream until finally they are faced with the cave entrance, a vast pit. Given that they have to abseil in, it is immediately apparent that this is not a 'tourist trap', but nobody questions at this stage whether or not this is actually Boreham Caverns. Holly may well have exaggerated its PG rating, and none of them, apart from Juno, has been here before.

Beth balks at the cave entrance, saying 'I'm an English teacher, not fucking Lara Croft!' in a dig at unrealistic action heroines. Juno organises the sequence for their descent, warning Holly not to pull any stunts, although predictably she comes down extremely quickly, then turns on her DV camera, which has an infra-red function. This introduces the idea of Holly being irresponsible, a risk-taker who won't follow orders, and the DV camera itself, which will come into its own later.

Sarah spots what look like claw marks on the walls, and is then caught up in a flight of bats flooding out from a crack in the cave wall. She panics and screams, and has to be calmed down by Juno; Holly, who responds by doing her best Count impersonation from *Sesame Street*, is told to 'fuck off' by Beth.

Juno states with authority that the only way out is to descend further into the convincingly claustrophobic 'pipe', which takes them into another vast chamber. Sarah thinks she's seen something and wanders off. Although there's no way she could have seen it, a particularly demonic-looking crawler is momentarily visible in a hollow beneath the women (at DVD timing 25:25). Holly is impressed by the cave, which gets a grin from Juno. The group takes a break, and Juno apologises to Sarah for not having stayed around after her accident. Sarah tells Juno that she feels 'a bit out of it' and that she's going to take a look around, revealing not only her mental state but also her rejection of a clear overture of friendship from Juno.

Sarah searches for and finds a passage that leads out of the cavern. Rebecca is mistrustful, and tells Juno that this isn't how she'd imagined it from the book; Juno responds that this is why she doesn't like books, 'too much room for interpretation'. Holly goes through the passage first, an extremely tight squeeze whose claustrophobic feel is enhanced by the sound design of the sequence, all clanking kit on the passage walls and panicked breathing, and the way it's filmed, with a handheld camera being pulled along the passage directly in front of the cavers.

Sarah, the last to enter the tunnel, hears what sounds like children laughing before she goes in. Beth is ahead of her, and stops when Sarah gets stuck. This sequence is harrowing less because of what happens than how it is depicted: Sarah's increasingly incoherent voice as she struggles, her breathing becoming more and more rapid and ragged; the camera ahead of her, still and slightly distant, so that she looks engulfed by the surrounding rock, giving the impression that she is simultaneously too small in relation to her surroundings and too large to pass through the passage, a nightmare vision from Wonderland.

The sound design adds to the visceral intensity of the scene, the clanking of the cavers' kit on the tunnel walls convincing us that we are watching steel on stone rather than flimsy plastic, while Sarah's panicked breathing in the tunnel ratchets up the tension to an unbearable degree.

Beth tells her that she needs to calm her breathing, and that the worst thing that could have happened to her has already happened; finally she tells her a joke, before they hear the tunnel beginning to collapse behind her. They abandon the rope bag that has been stuck behind her and make it through into the next chamber.

Sarah wakes from unconsciousness, via a shot of the out-of-focus birthday cake. None of the team is injured, although the tunnel collapse has filled the air with dust. Juno checks on Holly, who says 'Don't fucking touch me, I'm fine!' Rebecca says that according to the guidebook there are three exits from this cavern, forcing Juno to admit that she didn't bring the book. Rebecca has filed a flight plan for Boreham Caverns with Mountain Rescue, and accuses Juno of taking them into a different cave system. Juno, implicitly admitting this, says that Holly was right, Boreham Caverns is a tourist trap, prompting Holly to tell Juno not to 'pin this shit on me', and Rebecca to solemnly state 'This is not caving, this is an ego trip'. They are, of course, right to be angry with Juno: without consulting any of them, she has risked all of their lives going into an unknown system. She tries to defend herself on two points: that if there's no risk, there's no point, and that this is an unexplored system that they could discover themselves. How Juno has found out about this unexplored system is never clarified. Beth puts the boot in by berating Juno for leaving Sarah too soon after her accident; Juno states that 'We *all* lost something in that crash'.

The fault lines are clear now within the group. Juno has betrayed them by taking them into an unexplored system, in which they are now as good as trapped; she may also have betrayed Sarah with her husband. Yet we are not entirely unsympathetic: in some ways the situation resembles a tactless gift, offered with good intentions but sure to offend. In any case, Juno is not alone in shouldering responsibility for their situation: Sarah nominated the tunnel they used to leave the last cavern, and it is intimated that her struggle within the tunnel prompts its collapse, while she also left the rope bag behind.

The group is however experienced enough not to let the stress lines take over completely. They clear a passage through to something approaching an exit with their picks, only to find that they now have a chasm to cross. Rebecca insists on climbing across, putting pitons in the cave roof and laying a rope across so that the others can follow. Cue a scene of gruelling endurance, as Rebecca hangs from one hand while she tries to fetch a piton from her belt with the other, Juno barking orders at her all the while. The scene is lit using red flares, adding to a sense of something mythical about their trials and lending a distinctly underworld quality to the chasm. Nearing the passage on the far side of the chasm, Rebecca finds an antique piton wedged in the crack in the cave roof, into which she snaps a carabiner.

The others use the rope to make their way to the far side. Sarah and Juno are the last to cross. When they are alone Sarah asks, 'Was this about me or you?'

'It's about us. Getting back to what we used to be. I wanted us to claim this place, name it. I thought maybe your name.'

'Or maybe yours.'

This is an unexpectedly rich exchange. Sarah seems angry with Juno, although less for having taken them into an unexplored system than for some unspoken hostility that might relate to Juno's relationship to Paul. Juno's response suggests again that as a group they have begun to lose interest in adventure, or that they don't meet as much as previously, or, quite simply, that they are aging. 'Your name', for Sarah, is of course Paul's name, with its own clear appeal to Juno, even if squabbling over naming a cave when there is no certainty that you will emerge from it alive is slightly curious.

Juno is the last to cross the chasm and removes the pitons: with the other rope bag gone (an implicit dig at Sarah) she stresses that they will need all the equipment they can lay their hands on. This is also, of course, an attempt to out-climb Rebecca, a macho demonstration of skills. The demonstration doesn't quite go according to plan as Juno falls, whipping the rope through Rebecca's hands and slicing open her palm. This is the first blood spilled in the cave, and Rebecca's wound bears more than a passing resemblance to a bleeding vagina, adding to the intrauterine feel of the passages they have already moved through.

The antique piton, the last securing the rope, comes loose, and Juno slams against the chasm wall. She is shaken but uninjured, and is duly hauled up. They consider the piton, clear evidence that somebody has been there before them, although they think it's at least a hundred years old. Moving on they find more evidence of previous occupation in the form of a huge cave painting. Juno considers this irrelevant and encourages them to press on, but Beth insists they take a closer look at it and finds that it marks two exits.

Excited by the possibility of an exit, the group moves on, Julyan's score employing a heartbeat-paced bass pulse similar to Morricone's score for *The Thing*. We now have our first clear view of a crawler, albeit only in silhouette, drool dripping from its jaws. Its appearance in such close proximity to the discovery of the cave painting reinforces an association with something prehistoric.

At a split in the tunnels they use a lighter to test the wind direction. It sounds like a bonfire – a rare instance of the exaggerated physicality of the sound design shading into farce. Holly races down the 'correct' path, shrieking that she sees daylight. Juno runs after her, telling her to slow down, it's not daylight. Holly ignores her and slips into a hole in the ground, prompting one of the film's most distressing sequences. Juno manages to catch her before she falls through, but her grip on Holly's arm slips, Holly's eyes wide with panic in the darkness, until she falls. The music, which has been subtly foreboding through this entire sequence, cuts out immediately when she falls, leaving us only with the sounds of her bouncing off the cave walls and her groans of pain when she hits the bottom. Holly glances down with her head torch and discovers that she has broken her leg. Badly. Holly's realisation of what this means is superbly conveyed: shock, loss of mobility, the awareness that she will now be a burden on the team.

Again the professional reflexes kick in. The others know they need to get Holly out of there; her plight is almost a distraction from their own. Sam pushes the bone back in, a sickening sight, and equally squirm-inducing sound, then uses a pick as a splint to bind to her leg. While they attend to Holly, Sarah, distracted, hears what sounds like children laughing, and wanders off to investigate (shades of *Don't Look Now* [Nicolas Roeg, 1973]). She finds an antique helmet on the ground, and hears a clicking sound, like echolocation, around her, before seeing a white and naked figure in the distance. Juno catches up with her and Sarah is insistent that she's seen "a man", but nobody believes her. Juno explains that Holly had seen phosphorus on the rocks, which she'd mistaken for daylight: they are two miles underground.

They climb up into a large space full of bones, their first view of it like Kane's view of the Space Jockey in *Alien*. Holly is mobile, but barely, and clearly in great pain. Her DV camera has come in useful for scanning the scene, though – they can see the remains of hundreds of animals. Rebecca maintains that 'this is not good, guys', although at least it shows them that there's another way out – and that it's probably quite close. The first proper reveal of a crawler happens on the DV camera, as one looms into view behind them while they are screaming for help; we know it's coming, but it's still a shock. Sarah takes a perverse pleasure in their first sighting, as it reveals she'd been telling the truth all along, even if the others maintain that 'That was not a human being!'

Juno lights a yellow flare, which Sarah tells her to throw away, clearly worried that it will lead the crawlers to them. Juno acquiesces, following someone else's suggestion without query for the first time; but Sarah is wrong. The crawlers are blind and need no light, unlike the cavers, and after they douse their flare Sarah leads them directly into a crawler attack.

The injured Holly is the first to be attacked, the crawlers going straight for the neck, and Juno fights hard to stop her body being dragged away, burying her pick in one crawler with its hands on Holly then killing another that attacks Juno herself. In this kill frenzy Juno swings around, sensing something behind her, and digs her pick into Beth's neck. This is clearly accidental, and Juno is in shock, but Beth stares at her accusingly and grabs for Juno's pendant, tearing it from her neck before falling to the ground. Beth whispers, 'Don't leave me,' but Juno, clearly horrified, walks away. Juno can be forgiven for the mistaken identity: the attacks are completely disorienting, flashes of light and action, rapid edits and undercranking designed to convey an effect of confusion, at which they succeed perhaps too well.

The group has now split up, but the characters can be distinguished by the colours of light they use to navigate. Sarah, who has knocked herself out fleeing the crawlers, wakes up once again, after having a vision of the back of her daughter's head that morphs into a crawler, after she hears the whispered words 'If you're really ready'. She uses the infra-red function of the DV camera to find her way around, which also involves her being subjected to the sight of Holly's innards being eaten. She then cannibalises Holly herself, although only for usable kit: she takes the pick that had been used as a splint for her broken leg, wraps a rag around it, soaks it in petrol (they have petrol?) and sparks a flint to set it alight.

Meanwhile Sam and Rebecca, who are navigating the caves with a green glowstick, giving the cave a particularly eerie quality, narrowly avoid a crawler attack when the alarm on Sam's watch goes off, and Sam only just manages to throw it to the side in time. Julyan's musical cue brings to mind the Ligeti music used in the Dawn of Man sequence from 2001 (Stanley Kubrick, 1968), a film with its own points to make about caves, cavemen and evolution. Juno, who is navigating by a red flare that casts a hellish light over the cave, hears the alarm and comes to Sam's rescue as she is attacked again, twisting a crawler's head fully round. Rebecca spits on its corpse and Sam kicks it. Juno tells them that Beth is dead, but doesn't elaborate on the circumstances. The three take the opportunity to examine the crawler Juno has just killed, with Sam surmising that they are completely blind and probably use sound to hunt, having evolved to live in the dark.

Juno tells them that she has found chalk arrows presumably pointing towards an exit, but refuses to leave without Sarah. Meanwhile Sarah finds Beth, who is still alive underneath another body. Beth calls out for her and advises her to 'find your own way out' rather than looking for Juno, as Juno 'did this to me'. Sarah clearly finds this difficult to accept, until Beth hands her the pendant she'd torn from Juno's neck. Sarah reads the inscription 'Love each day', confirming her suspicion that Juno and Paul had an inappropriately close relationship. Beth asks Sarah to kill her, which Sarah does – reluctantly – by bringing a rock down on her friend's head.

Sarah is now attacked by a particularly small crawler, which she dispatches quickly. A female crawler – with long hair and naked breasts – finds the crawler she's just killed (presumably this is one of her children) and chases her until she falls into a deep pool of blood. Her slow emergence from the pool is a clear nod to *Apocalypse Now* (Francis Ford Coppola, 1979). There is an odd hiatus, a moment of calm in an otherwise frenetically paced sequence, as she emerges, before the female crawler attacks again. Sarah scrabbles around for a weapon and finds a tusk which she buries in the crawler's eye. Another crawler appears and Sarah plays dead as it moves over her, dripping mucus from its jaws onto her face. When the crawler is safely past she screams.

Juno hears a scream and wants to wait for Sarah, but Rebecca tells her that she must be dead. Juno runs her torch over a large group of crawlers in an *Aliens*-style reveal, and follows Rebecca and Sam to the chasm they'd crossed before. Sam tries to climb across but is attacked halfway over; she manages to stab one crawler but is attacked by another, which tears out her throat. Rebecca is pulled back down the tunnel she'd just come from to have her belly ripped apart. Juno jumps and lands in the water below, only to be attacked by the crawler Sam had stabbed. She kills him then climbs up the chasm wall, and is pulled into the far tunnel entrance by Sarah, who looks so deranged – spattered in blood, *Carrie*-style, and wild-eyed – that Juno's 'what happened to you?' is as much about her appearance as about where she'd been. This sequence highlights a problem with the score; when it is occasionally difficult to distinguish from the film's sound effects. When Juno climbs up the cave wall after jumping into the chasm we can hear echoing sounds like sonar blips, which could just about be ambient sounds of the cave; when she subsequently meets Sarah the screeching strings sound a lot like crawler screams.

Sarah asks Juno about the others, including the following exchange:

Sarah: 'What about Beth?'

Juno: 'Didn't make it.'

Sarah: 'You saw her die?'

Juno nods.

The two move on, and find the other entrance to the cave. Sarah is armed, like Juno, with a pick; given that when we last saw her she only had a torch – she throws her tusk away after the pool scene – this may well be a continuity error. They are attacked, and respond with shocking ferocity. Sarah bites one crawler then buries her thumbs in another's eyes, *Evil Dead*-style, for far longer than it would take to kill it. Juno slams a crawler head against a rock then buries a pick in another's skull. They have killed the only crawlers present but Sarah, dangling the pendant from her hand, half-smiles, half-grimaces at Juno and buries her pick in Juno's knee. Juno pulls the pick out and turns to face a new group of crawlers.

Sarah falls down a tunnel and finds herself in the boneyard, where she passes out. When she comes to she can see daylight, and crawls up a slope of bones to emerge in the woods beyond, her hands reaching out from beneath the leaves in a nod to the iconic publicity shot for *The Evil Dead*. She runs screaming through the woods, gets into the SUV and drives away. On the road she pauses to be sick, then sees a ghostly vision of Juno in the seat next to her.

She screams and comes to again, now face down on the ground in the cave, although she no longer seems to be in the boneyard. We can see light flickering on her face, light from the birthday cake we can now see in focus before her, with Jessica on the far side; we hear a very faint 'Mummy' before Jessica offers her the cake. The camera pans back to Sarah, looking beatifically at her daughter, then pulls away, showing that she is sitting alone with her flaming torch in front of her, in a hollow with the sounds of crawlers all around her.

THE SHOCK OF THE OLD

Progress? What a Belgian idea. Baudelaire

Horror is the most atavistic of genres. We live in a rational, scientific world, in which belief in the supernatural has been consigned to the dustbin of history, fairy tales for those unable to accept the unforgiving realities of materialism, yet we flock to see tales of unquiet spirits or possession by demons. Most of us work in offices and lead lives in thrall to corporate pressures and market forces, having traded in risk and autonomy for physical security and the promise of a regular wage; but we love films whose characters are forced to fend for themselves, to fight for their survival in a wilderness bereft of emergency services or even a friendly neighbour.

Horror recognises the allure of the past, figured variously as either pre-Enlightenment or pre-industrial, but tends to conceive of it only in the bloodiest, most violent terms. During a horror film we may be allowed temporarily to believe in the supernatural, to subscribe to a pre-Enlightenment world view; but this supernatural will only display itself in the most appallingly vile manifestations. We may be allowed temporarily to hanker after a bucolic, pastoral past, the pre-industrial landscapes of English pagan horror films like *Blood on Satan's Claw* (Piers Haggard, 1970), *Matthew Hopkins, Witchfinder General* (Michael Reeves, 1968) or even *The Wicker Man* (Robin Hardy, 1973); but this nostalgia, this Romanticism, is tempered by a Hobbesian conviction that life, outside modernity, was for the majority nasty, brutish and short.

The nostalgia is driven by a dissatisfaction with modern life, an urge to live closer to a state of nature, untrammelled by the bounds of civilisation. The dissatisfaction is understandable: living standards, in the West at least, continue to rise but are conceived solely in terms of life expectancy and access to consumer goods, with little attention paid to the less quantifiable factors of the intensity and fulfilment of the fully lived life. A prevalent anomie is only worsened by the increasingly unavoidable realisation that our demand for cheap consumer goods drives environmental and human devastation around the globe. The idea of progress, always a shaky concept for the heathens being enforcibly 'civilised' by their colonial masters, now seems almost entirely untenable, its dominance as the central discourse of Western civilisation increasingly replaced by a discourse of decline embodied variously in the figures of the feral chav, the illegal immigrant and, in an explosive return of the religious repressed, the fundamentalist Islamic terrorist

As if the inescapable awareness of the consequences of our actions were not enough, in the scramble for a security always already undercut by our own mortality we have lost something, or, as Lewis (Burt Reynolds) claims in *Deliverance* – a key influence on *The Descent* – sold something, trading in our ability to survive without the trappings of civilised life for the comforts of air conditioning. Yet even Lewis, poster boy for a post-apocalyptic survivalism, finds that the reality of his canoe trip doesn't quite live up to his Romantic valorisation of nature. Sickening compound fractures and deranged hillbillies were never part of Lewis's script, even if he does enjoy the opportunity to put an arrow through a man's back.

The reliability with which 'back to nature' narratives go wrong in what has been called the urbanoia subgenre kicked off by *Deliverance* might hint at an innate conservatism to these films, a subtextual message that 'Yes, we know it looks good too, but trust us, you're better off staying at home'. Such conservatism would explain in part the commercial appeal of these films, in an increasingly urbanised world. Here we can have our cake and eat it: we can enjoy the look of the great outdoors, the vicarious thrill of living outside the system, but finally be happy that we are sitting comfortably in a cinema watching some poor fool be raped by a mountain man or eaten by a bear, safe in the knowledge that we have done the sensible thing by not braving the wilds ourselves.

Alternatively, and perhaps more convincingly, the bummer arcs of these films speak to our uncomfortable awareness that our Romantic preconceptions of nature are based on an illusion. To the kinds of people who live 'close to nature' – the remaining hunter-gatherer societies of the world – such a conception of nature is completely alien. For nature to be a refuge from civilisation, indeed for it to have any kind of value at all as a concept, we need to be outside it, separate; to view nature as valuable, we have to be irreparably severed from it. The trajectory is one way; not only can we never return, but our alienation prompts us to load the concept of nature with an insupportable weight of associations that we rarely recognise as being expressions of our own human need rather than essential qualities of the natural environment.

***

The decision to go on a caving trip, putting their lives in danger for a leisure activity, suggests that the group in *The Descent* considers modern life soft and unchallenging. Beth's is the only job mentioned, but it is difficult to imagine Juno and Holly knuckling down to a 9–5 office job, chatting about last night's TV around the water cooler. They are driven to test themselves in ways otherwise unavailable to them in modern life; they want adrenalin kicks and the best way they have found to get them is through extreme sports.

The desire to return, if only temporarily, to a more challenging environment is in a sense a desire to return to the past. Crucially on this trip they are going into a cave, emblematic of the distant past and symbolic of the womb, the unconscious and nature as opposed to culture. They are, however, prepared: they are well equipped with high-tech kit, including clothes that smooth over their feminine forms, giving them what critic Barbara Creed terms 'clean and proper bodies', 'fully symbolic' bodies that 'bear no indication of [their] debt to nature' (1993:11), making this in principle a very controlled, technological descent into the past. Indeed they are going in to incorporate the cave into culture. It is an unexplored system, as Juno belatedly reveals to the others, and she plans to name it, to bring it inside language, the symbolic order.

They also take a DV camera with them and film the expedition. While this serves several functions on a narrative level – it can record in infra-red light, allowing them to see in the dark, and adds a *Blair Witch*-style sense of authenticity to the proceedings – it also demonstrates that they are not living in the moment at all. The crawlers don't seem to have culture; the cavers are inextricably embedded in it. They want to record events for posterity, and for other people to see what they've done; rather than simply living the experience in its immediacy, they are already thinking about the future (and indeed the DV footage plays a central role in the sequel) – how will the expedition be remembered?

While Juno expects this to be an unexplored system, they find evidence that others have been there before them – hundred-year-old climbing equipment, a helmet and a cave painting. The cave painting appears to offer them crucial information, indicating that archaic skills would be of more use than a reliance on modern technology. Elsewhere they use the flame on a lighter to judge air direction in a tunnel, and Sarah's battery-powered torch is eventually replaced by its flaming equivalent. She later finds that a tusk makes an adequate replacement as a weapon for a pick – it's even the same size and shape, giving the disorienting impression that objects themselves are regressing to their Palaeolithic forebears. Finally she regresses beyond any kind of tool use at all, learning that biting and judiciously placed thumbs work as well as any other way of killing a crawler. Modern technology may even put the group at risk, as when the alarm on a watch alerts a crawler to their presence.

Obviously things don't go as planned: a nasty leg-break illustrates the impossibility of a technological fix for the vulnerability of the body, and the discovery of the crawlers takes the group straight back to a past in which people were prey. Nature here may not be the extreme sports arena they'd envisaged, but it remains a testing ground for them.

The film's descent into the past goes deeper than this, marking a quest for origins on a number of levels. Such a quest can be seen as motivated by Sarah's condition, grief-stricken enough a year after the death of her husband and child to remain on medication, suggesting a desire to start again, to set the counter back to zero. For Juno the trip is 'about getting back to what we used to be'. The implication is that as adventure sports enthusiasts they are out of practice, though the comment applies more broadly: they 'used to be', in species terms, more instinctual and savage; ultimately they 'used to be' undifferentiated from the mother by the fact of having been in the womb. *The Descent* explores both of these forms of regression. So there is a biological return to origins: the intrauterine imagery throughout the film and the trajectory of the group through the cave system suggest a theme of rebirth and a return to the womb. The return is also cultural: the group's encounter with the crawlers can be seen as analogous to the prehistoric competition between modern Homo sapiens and Neanderthals, while Sarah and Juno's descent into brutality marks a return to a state of instinctual savagery, untrammelled by the rules of civilisation. And the return is also psychical, Sarah's madness figured as a kind of splitting that undoes the illusory coherence of the ego, while her psychosis reminds us of the limitations of modern subjectivity.

GOING UNDERGROUND

I always wanted to do a horror film set in a cave. It's the classic environment. Horror films are best set in the dark, and you won't get any more dark than this. Neil Marshall, 'The Making of *The Descent*'

Caves present such obvious advantages to horror film-makers, it's surprising that *The Descent* is one of the few genre films set almost entirely inside one. Yet some of the advantages – they are entirely credible dark, confined spaces – may be disadvantages from a practical point of view: real caves present problems in terms of lighting and power access more generally, while insurers would probably balk at the idea of cast and crew members slipping around deep underground. Marshall suggested as much in an interview with *Film Threat* magazine (in Campos 2006):

> We knew from very early into production that we couldn't shoot this film in real caves. It'd be too expensive, too dangerous, too impractical, not to mention time consuming and we'd either have to find a cave that would fit the action in the script, or write the action based around the cave, so it was never going to work.

These technical problems probably account in part for the rash of cave films that came out around the same time as *The Descent* – *The Cave*, *The Cavern* and *Caved In: Prehistoric Terror* (Richard Pepin, 2006): set-building technology and CGI had finally made caves fully viable locations in which to set a film.

Technical hiccups notwithstanding, caves feature in passing in countless horror films. They are the lair of monsters in everything from *King Kong* (Marian C. Cooper, 1933) to *Trolljegeren/Trollhunter* (André Øvredal, 2010), the hideaway for vampires in films as disparate as *Der Fluch der grünen Augen/Cave of the Living Dead* (Ákos Ráthonyi, 1964) and *The Lost Boys* (Joel Schumacher, 1987) and the default home of the cannibal tribes of films like *Ultimo mondo cannibale/Last Cannibal World* (Ruggero Deodato, 1977) and *La montagna del dio cannibale/Mountain of the Cannibal God* (Sergio Martino, 1978). They even provide the location of an alien spaceship that doubles as a Bigfoot production line, in *Demonwarp* (Emmett Alston, 1988). Most of these films feature caves only in passing, or as backdrops with only the sketchiest use of their symbolic associations. Lengthier cave visits are restricted to the likes of *Alien Terror*, bucking a trend by keeping its characters inside what looks like a real cave system for the bulk of its running time; insurance must be cheaper in Italy.

Disused mine shafts and man-made tunnels feature more heavily than caves in horror – the discovery of a secret network of tunnels behind a facade of normality is a horror staple from the earliest Gothic novels to the modern horror film, visible in everything from *The Phantom of the Opera* (Rupert Julian, 1925) to *Martyrs* (Pascal Laugier, 2008) – and tend to be explored at greater length, perhaps for the technical reasons outlined above. They share certain qualities with caves, as do all subterranean spaces: the cellar, the sewer, the pit, the subway, the catacomb, the crypt.

Firstly, and perhaps most importantly, they are *dark*, providing the principal fear that *The Descent* plays on, perhaps the most primal fear of all. Marshall's insistence that only natural lighting sources should be used makes for some inventive lighting solutions and occasional confusion: in the darkness it can be difficult to tell one character from another (Sarah and Sam look particularly similar under their hard hats) and indeed exactly what's going on – when Sarah scavenges Holly's body for usable kit it's unclear exactly what she uses to make her flaming torch. These problems, along with the fact that for much of the film most of the frame is completely black, make the decision to use only what looks like a facsimile of natural lighting a bold one; but it works. The viewer is reduced to a childlike state of fear faced with the engulfing, smothering darkness. That the darkness should hide something as grotesque as the crawlers only adds to the sense of infantile nightmare.

But darkness is only half the story. Cinematic underworlds are multivalent spaces, able equally to represent a social underground or a character's psyche, and all points in between. They are places where the overground rules no longer apply, the chthonic realm. They are entrances to the underworld, the womb, the unconscious. And crucially they are not only mythic but material. As David Pike explains in a discussion of the subterranean tunnels of *The Third Man* (Carol Reed, 1949):

> Like the logic of myth from which popular cinema inherited much of its subterranean tropes, the descent into the underworld is a privileged moment in the narrative arc, a moment of danger and revelation, of death and return. But this mythic resonance is

only part of the cinematic underworld, for one of the defining qualities of Reed and Greene's sewers, despite the satanic undertone in Lime's character, is their resolute materiality. They are an other world in the medieval sense of a space of adventure that follows different rules than the ordered world above, but they are also a physical world of brick and mortar that any member of the audience could visit, or could imagine visiting, should they so desire. (2009: 317-8)

Caves add something further to the mix: they are both natural and ancient, unfamiliar yet familiar, hostile yet not without grandeur and beauty, aligning them with the undersea world and space. Yet their associations are far more specific. The characters in *The Descent* – indeed in any cave horror film – are oppressed by the crushing weight not only of several thousand tons of rock around them but also with the overloaded symbolic freight of the cave, and its several millennia worth of mythic associations.

For our earliest ancestors they must have represented shelter, protection from the elements and predators; that they also represented something magical or sacred seems likely from the animal/human hybrids common to cave paintings around the world. Some have argued that the paintings of Lascaux and Chauvet in France are evidence of prehistoric shamanic activity, hallucinations fixed in space; the feeling of entering a cave is itself said to be common on crossing the threshold of intense hallucinatory states, as though the vision of a tunnel or vortex were neurologically hardwired into the human brain (see **Nightmares in a Damaged Brain**).

For us the associations with prehistory remain: we think of 'cavemen', and caves bear a modern association with evolution, whether in terms of speculation about the dawn of man or exaggerated evolutionary trajectories, whether downsliding (enforced stays in caves tend to make people eat each other, at least according to the movies – see **One Million Years BC**) or sideways mutations, as in *The Cave*. They are also an alien, unknown space capable of harbouring Lovecraftian monstrosities, such as those in *The Boogens* (James L. Conway, 1981) or *The Strangeness* (Melanie Anne Phillips, 1985), or serving as the perfect backdrop to *Alien Terror*'s gory tale of alien invasion.

According to Florence Weinberg in *The Cave*, by the time of Classical civilisations caves had come to represent unrefined nature and a state of ignorance rather than shelter, pictured most succinctly and famously, perhaps, in Plato's image of people watching shadows on the wall of a cave and mistaking them for reality. For Plato the cave was something that needed to be escaped, transcended, in favour of the light outside.

Other Classical myths of the cave played on a relay of associations – the cave could be nurturing, educational; it might represent an escape from the world, a retreat from the cares of everyday life. The womblike qualities of the cave were characteristically however portrayed as a lure, a trap: however nurturing a cave might be, like the womb it would eventually have to be left. To remain in the womb of the cave, however tempting, is to court death in the 'womb-tomb': to remain in the womb risks being reassimilated, losing one's identity, being devoured.

For Weinberg cave associations in Western culture remained relatively static until the Romantics, who also associated the cave with nature but reversed the polarity of the Classical equation. For them society had become over-refined; they drew on Rousseau's idea of the noble savage to suggest that with socialisation something key to human nature had been lost. For them nature 'becomes a means of universal salvation, the state to which man hungers to return as noble savage or as renegade from society ... The Romantic nostalgia for the "blessed" simplicity of the forefathers, a nostalgia still obvious in the twentieth century, resembles the perennial wish for a return to Eden, to the state of purity before the Fall' (Weinberg 1986: 294).

Caves are classically also gateways to the underworld, key locations in the myths of descent into the underworld, death and rebirth that are central to so many myth cycles: the Greek legend of Orpheus and Eurydice, for example, or the Norse legend of Baldr and Hermóôr or the Sumerian Gilgamesh's descent to meet Utnapishtim.

Which of these associations is at work in Marshall's film? The cave is approached principally as a location for adventure, sport, although its association with the nurturing womb is implicitly invoked in the idea that the trip might help Sarah to cope with her grief, quite apart from the womb and birth imagery suffusing the film. The cave raises questions about evolution: the cavers see a cave painting, necessarily reminding them of their far-distant ancestors, and encounter a group of relict hominids who want to eat them, and who appear to have followed an evolutionary path unique to this cave system. And the women themselves change, shedding the niceties of civilisation and returning to a state of savagery. While Juno manages to retain a sense of common humanity in her bid to rescue Sarah at the end, against her friends' protestations, Sarah shows that she has fully rejected any social concerns by wounding Juno, demonstrating her inability to transcend or leave the cave.

The Romantic valorising of nature over culture underpins the expedition's aims: modern life lacks challenges – at least physical challenges – and the very modern form of adventure tourism engaged in by the cavers is in part a desire to return to a closeness to nature, a stripping away of the redundant accretions of social, civilised life. There is also a Romantic sense in the film of the limitations of rationality and materialism: how can these help us to deal with grief, with the confrontation with death? The cave represents nature in its cycle of death and rebirth, but also represents the abyss, the void, the limits of knowledge. With the hallucinatory nature of Sarah's experiences (explored in **Nightmares in a Damaged Brain**), *The Descent* mobilises nearly all of the cave associations cited above.

ONE MILLION YEARS BC

My theory was these were the cavemen who stayed in the cave. The rest came out and evolved and became the human race. These went into the cave and evolved and adapted and became these cave creatures. So they are human. They're just an offshoot of the human race. I wanted to apply that logic to the way that they looked. If they'd been living underground for thousands of years, the pigment in their skin's changed. They're blind. They use their smell and their hearing to hunt. They've got a sonar capacity like bats. They've really adapted, scuttling around the caves. And I just thought we'd apply that to the way they were going to look and behave. There was initially, at least in the first cut of the film, a brief scene where one of the characters attempted to guess this, to explain this. And we cut it out because I thought it was better to leave this ambiguous. We didn't need to explain too much. But that's my story. Neil Marshall, Comic-Con 2006 interview

Marshall's comment justifies the absence from the finished film of any categorical explanation for the crawlers. His point is fair: by refusing to foreclose any potential explanation through a privileging of one particular story, the film leaves its options open, and the viewer wondering. Marshall may have explained the crawlers' origins in interviews, but he is always at pains to couch this as *his* theory, *his* story – there may be others.

Marshall used theatrical actors (including Craig Conway, a regular in his films) for the crawlers, rather than CGI, making for painstaking and lengthy make-up work. Part of the rationale behind this is to differentiate the crawlers as individuals, to give them distinguishing features. I'm not convinced this works – the darkness makes it difficult enough to tell the cavers apart, let alone the crawlers – but the sense of them as a kind of generic mass only adds to their iconic, low-mythic qualities.

Sam, the medical student, does subject a crawler to the kind of quasi-scientific examination that has long been a staple of the horror film: think of similar scenes in *Alien* and *The Thing*. From studying their eyes – blind – and the shape of their ears, Sam concludes that they hunt using echolocation, like bats, explaining the clicking sounds they make. Their sense of smell seems patchy, despite Marshall's comments above. The mother crawler sniffs at her child and seems able to tell that it is dead; but elsewhere the crawlers routinely come sniffingly close to the cavers without sensing them – all the cavers have to do to avoid detection is stay still.

This highlights another technical problem with the crawlers. If they 'see' using echolocation, the fight scenes should be full of the sound of their clicking as they try to work out where the cavers are. But the crawlers are more or less silent during the fights: they simply seem to know automatically the location of their prey. If their hearing alone is acute enough for them to sense the topography of their environment, then it should allow them to hear the cavers' breath and even heartbeats, but the crawlers evidently can't hear them unless the cavers move. By this token the crawlers should be knocking themselves out by running into the cave walls when they stop clicking. Perhaps, as Barbara Creed suggests, monsters represent 'the point where meaning collapses' (2005: xvii-xviii).

Such technical fussing aside, we see that not only their hunting by sound but also their snub, pushed-up noses, pointy, triangulate ears and their environment itself align them with bats. This alignment recalls vampires, and the crawlers share more than just this with horror's most celebrated monster. Their two pointy front teeth and their ghostly pallor are reminiscent of the eponymous vampire in both versions of Nosferatu (F.W. Murnau, 1922 and Werner Herzog, 1979), a point raised by special make-up effects designer Paul Hyett in the 'making of' documentary. They also – which Hyett fails to mention – bear more than a passing resemblance to the Reaper vampires in Blade II (Guillermo del Toro, 2002) and Gollum of Peter Jackson's Lord of the Rings trilogy (2001–03). They share other vampiric qualities too: we can assume from their blindness that they only leave the cave to hunt at night, and their pigmentation may even make exposure to the sun problematic. They also attack necks, in classic vampire fashion, although they are partial to bellies too, being cannibalistic.

Aside from their vampiric qualities, the crawlers represent what the cavers can only ever aspire to, an instinctual state of nature. No romanticised vision of nature, either, or one of it as some vast sports arena, as per the cavers' assumptions: here it is red in tooth and claw. The crawlers appear to have no culture, no tools, not even any knowledge of fire; they have no need to seek out adventure to throw off what the cavers evidently view as the oppressive shackles of civilised life. The cavers have to rely on ropes and complicated climbing equipment – the products of a highly industrialised culture – to make their way through the caves; the crawlers don't need any of that *kit*. The cavers can't even defend themselves without tools until close to the end, when Juno and Sarah adopt a more hands-on approach to their aggressors.

The crawlers have been seen by some critics as embodiments of a monstrous patriarchy. When Sarah first spots one she tells the others that she's seen 'a man', suggesting such an alignment; the later, unexpected appearance of a female crawler suggests that the crawlers follow traditional (read: patriarchal) gender roles, with the males out hunting and the females tending the young.

The cavers' disparate nationalities may be relevant in entertaining yet another notion about the crawlers. Sarah is Scottish, Beth English and Holly Irish, while Sam and Rebecca appear to be Scandinavian, perhaps Swedish, and while Juno speaks with an American accent she is of Eurasian stock; this is a fairly accurate representation of early immigrant cultures in the US. The crawlers are, by contrast, native, indigenous, 'American' in a way that no immigrant could ever hope to be. In this sense – particularly with the inclusion of the rock art in the cave – the crawlers can be seen as representing the indigenous people of the US – in the colonial framework they are savage, alien and prolific, protecting their environment from interlopers bearing shiny metal tools.

A sense of displacement – of guilt translating into demonisation – may be operating here, as with a theory that sees the crawlers symbolising another 'first people', the Neanderthals. They do not, granted, resemble what we know of Neanderthals: the heavy brow, low forehead, powerful jaw and build are all lacking, while Neanderthals are also presumed to have had hair. But there has been speculation about Neanderthal survivals into modern times, particularly in remote parts of Siberia, and we are known to have shared the planet with them for thousands of years, anatomically modern Homo sapiens coming to supplant them during the period known as the Upper Palaeolithic Transition, between 45 and 35,000 years ago. (Neanderthals are classified alternately as a subspecies of Homo sapiens – Homo sapiens neanderthalis – or as an entirely separate human species – Homo neanderthalis. For convenience subsequent references to 'anatomically modern Homo sapiens' will be shortened to 'Homo sapiens' on the understanding that this does *not* include Neanderthals.) This period saw huge leaps forward in language, art, tool-making and the complexity of burial rites: the great networks of cave paintings at places like Lascaux and Chauvet in France are dated to this period.

The presence of a cave painting – a large, detailed painting, moreover – in *The Descent* suggests that an examination of this transition period is not irrelevant to understanding the film. The painting is interpreted as a map by Beth, the schoolteacher, perhaps erroneously, given that whatever else the paintings of animals and beast-headed men in Lascaux or Chauvet were, they were not maps.

There are also technical problems with the cave painting. Such a style, familiar from Chauvet and Lascaux, is a European tradition; the North American tradition is more Asian-influenced and was usually done in rock shelters. It's unclear, too, who has done this painting. Cave painting is a clear mark of culture, of an ability to understand representational art. The crawlers don't appear to have culture; they don't even have *fire*. If their ancestors had done the painting, why should they have reached this point of achievement and then begun to devolve? This looks like an oversight on Marshall's part, a small point easily lost in the ensuing frenzy – but as an interpretive tool the painting may still be useful to us.

David Lewis-Williams advances an explanation for the relationship between cave painting and what has been termed the 'Creative Explosion' in the Upper Paleolithic period in *The Mind in the Cave*. He argues that the archaeological evidence shows that Neanderthals could borrow only certain forms of technology from Homo sapiens – certain forms of tool making and burial rites – and that others, including complex language and representational art, were beyond them. The recognition by groups of Homo sapiens of the limitations of Neanderthal consciousness was, for Lewis-Williams, the spur for the 'Creative Explosion', by fostering a social stratification between the two groups that led to an increased competitiveness and the possibility of forms of social oppression:

> Art and ritual may well contribute to social cohesion, but they do so by marking off groups from other groups and thus creating the potential for social tensions. It was not co-operation but social competition and tension that triggered an ever-widening

spiral of social, political and technological change that continued long after the last Neanderthal had died. (2002: 95)

Cave paintings, for Lewis-Williams, mark social divisiveness, the recognition that 'we' (Homo sapiens) can make and understand this, while 'you' (Neanderthals) cannot.

What relevance might this have for *The Descent*? I have mentioned the atavism key to the film, and to horror more generally; allied to this is a search for origins, a return to the source – here, of human culture, dawning during the 'Creative Explosion', arguably the result of oppression of Neanderthals by Homo sapiens.

Of course, the crawlers hardly seem to represent an oppressed group, picking their way with relative ease through the far more technologically advanced cavers. In this respect, though, they may be subject to the same kind of displacement that Carol Clover lists as typical of the demonisation of the hillbilly villains of urbanoia films like *Deliverance*. There the city men are aware of their guilt, their responsibility for the dam which will flood the river, uprooting entire communities; but their guilt is displaced or assuaged by a conviction that the hillbillies are subhuman, grotesque, whether through in-breeding or through their breaking of taboos (in *Deliverance*, sexual taboos). *The Hills Have Eyes* (Wes Craven, 1977) displays a similar displacement of urban guilt through a focus on the dietary taboo of cannibalism on the part of the feral family, a feature shared by *The Descent*. According to critic Mikita Brottman, in her study of cannibalism in the cinema, *Meat is Murder*:

> The regular strategy of rejection, according to anthropology, starts with the libel, whether this be the simple food libel (the libelled group eats disgusting foods), the sex libel (the demeaned category is promiscuous, effeminate or incestuous), to [sic] the blood libel (the demeaned category is murderous and – ultimately – cannibalistic). (1998: 67)

By this reading, then, one of the meanings carried by the crawlers is that they represent the Neanderthals, our close cousins who died out some 30,000-odd years ago. The crawlers are represented as vicious, violent and cannibalistic to displace guilt over their disappearance through their portrayal in the worst possible light. One feature of the film tending to support such a reading is, conversely, a certain sympathy shown towards them, as with the underdogs or monsters in all of Marshall's films. They are, as Marshall has pointed out in interviews, simply defending their territory – and bringing home the bacon at the same time – instinctual, necessary processes far removed from the decadent adventuring indulged in by the cavers. Sarah's slaying of a child crawler, and its mother's subsequent attack on her, are further designed to trouble our easy equation of crawler=monster.

An obvious criticism of this argument is that nobody remembers what happened 35,000-odd years ago: how could there be guilt attached to the idea of Homo sapiens' mistreatment of Neanderthals, an idea that is, in any case, speculative? One answer is that however it happened, the coexistence of Homo sapiens and Neanderthals was followed by the extinction of the latter group: *something* happened to the Neanderthals, something that we might associate with Western mistreatment of first peoples more generally, from Native Americans to Australian Aboriginals and Amazonian tribespeople.

Some writers on horror also posit transgenerational or racial sources of fear. H.P. Lovecraft, for whom tales of subterranean regression were something of a stock in trade – 'The Lurking Fear' and 'The Rats in the Walls' both feature creatures that prefigure the crawlers – specialised in a kind of 'cosmic fear' that 'reaches back towards humankind's dawn and thus constitutes a transgenerational phenomenon' (Cavallero 2002: 16). Lafcadio Hearn (in Cavallero, ibid.) expressed the similar idea that: 'Elements of primeval fears – fears older than humanity – doubtless enter into the child-terror of darkness' and 'fears of ghosts may very possibly be composed with inherited results of ... ancestral experience of nightmare.'

We can also simply take the monsters at face value. They are cavemen and they like to eat people. Perhaps they represent another evolutionary branch, as in Marshall's explanation, recalling the notion, explored in folklore, fantastic fiction – think of Arthur Machen's 'little people' – and cryptozoology, that we continue to share the planet with other near-humans. The idea underpins the Bigfoot cycle of horror films spurred by the cryptozoological mania of the 1970s, which even managed to spawn one genuine video nasty in 1980's *Night of the Demon* (James C. Wasson), an amateurish if entertainingly splashy entry whose chief claim to fame is showing a biker's penis being ripped off by a bush-dwelling Bigfoot. The creature's violence here is senseless insofar as it is not looking for food; for relict hominids with a taste for human flesh we need to turn to *The Pit* (Lew Lehman, 1981) (see **Family**). But the Bigfoot reference made early in *The Descent* is something of a red herring: the crawlers are more recognisably human than the ape-like missing links that populate the various Bigfoot films.

Perhaps, conversely, the crawlers were once like us, maybe even a previous caving expedition, but regressed, or adapted to life in the cave without ever seeing a need to leave. Caves, after all, characteristically represent a site of devolution, a sliding down the evolutionary ladder marked by cannibalistic desires. Consider – even if his tube tunnels are not *quite* caves – the fate of the Man (Hugh Armstrong) in *Death Line* (Gary Sherman, 1973) (see **Family**), or the caving party in *The Severed Arm* (Thomas S. Alderman, 1973), who draw straws after a cave-in to see whose arm gets eaten.

Colqhoun (Robert Carlyle) in *Ravenous* also finds that being holed up in a cave fills him with an irresistible urge to taste human flesh, although for him cannibalism leads to a vigour quite unlike the Man's piteous whimperings or the guilty fears of *The Severed Arm*'s cavers, each convinced that he will be the next to suffer a vengeful limb-lopping.

Even living in the space between two rocks can be enough to guarantee a partiality to human flesh: the irradiated family of *The Hills Have Eyes* have a hankering for the Carters' 'tenderloin baby', although it won't go very far between them. Inveterate social climber Ruby (Janus Blythe) wants to leave the world of roast kid and matted furs behind, showing her snobbery early in the film by refusing to eat Beauty, the Carters' dog. Her resentful embrace of aspirational culture seals her family's fate as she rescues the baby, allowing the Carters to indulge in a frenzy of vengeful violence that represents as much of an atavistic throwback as *The Descent*'s eye-gougings and ear-bitings.

At least these cave cannibals are recognisably human. By the time no-nonsense archaeologist Dr Bentley (a typically earnest John Agar) discovers *The Mole People*, an ancient Sumerian civilisation that collapsed long in the past into a cave system during an earthquake, its slave population has regressed into a peculiarly 1950s American form of monstrosity, with bugged-out eyes and two-pronged claws that make them scaly cousins of *This Island Earth*'s (Joseph M. Newman, 1955) Metaluna Monster. The Mole People, presumably so named for their ability to burrow into the soft earth at will, are cannibals, and prey on their human masters, but Bentley, whose main concern is to seduce a Sumerian waitress before his torch batteries run out, glosses over their dietary tastes and provokes a slave revolt. *The Mole People*, inspired by H.G. Wells and countless crackpot theories about hollow earths, including the wilder excesses of Richard Shaver and Stanislav Szukalski, turns *The Time Machine* on its head: here the cannibal monsters are the good guys, and Bentley is all for them enjoying a sumptuous Sumerian feast.

What Waits Below (Don Sharp, 1985) picks up the lost civilisation ball and fumbles it badly. A US military team hires unlikely mercenary Clayton 'Wolf' Wolfson (Robert Powell) to place a radio transmitter inside an unexplored Belizean cave system. The caves are, of course, inhabited – by a gang of albinos purporting to be Mayans and an inexplicable black snakelike thing. The Mayans, whose hearing has become acutely sensitive after centuries underground, can hear the transmitter, and naturally object to its presence; 'Wolf', no great fan of the military's plan, just wants to get his archaeologist friends out of the system safe and sound.

The Time Machine's Morlocks have, like the Mole People, regressed to subhuman levels through their retreat into a cave system in the wake of an apocalyptic war. The Eloi, who have remained on the surface, enjoy an idyllic life of responsibility-free play, gambolling in the fields and lakes while the Morlocks feed and clothe them and occasionally dispatch a few of them for food. The Eloi appear to have conquered what might be considered a substantial drawback to being human: awareness of mortality. The trade-off, then, doesn't sound too bad: no wage slavery for the Eloi, who remain unfazed by their companions' occasional disappearance, presumably to end up on a Morlock plate. It is this carefree attitude to life, rather than their culinary fate, that incenses George (Rod Taylor) in George Pal's 1967 film of Wells's novel: demonstrating a characteristically colonial urge to interfere, George shatters the Eloi's world and kills as many Morlocks as he can before speeding back to his own time – although his heart may have been won by a simple Eloi smile.

RETURN TO THE SOURCE

Other people have come up with stories, which kind of is intentional, about it being a kind of journey back into the womb. The slimy dark passages with little white guys running around. The blood cave. It's all in there. A lot of it was deliberate because it occurred to me while we were making it. I was designing passages that looked like various orifices and things like that. Neil Marshall in Stax, 2006

There's only one way out of this chamber and that's down the pipe. Juno

Why does Sarah want to go on the caving expedition in the first place? The others think the trip will do her good: it's been a year since the death of Paul and Jessica, and the expedition is a way of welcoming her back into their community. It's not clear, though, that Sarah is ready to be welcomed back: she is taking pills, presumably for anxiety, or perhaps anti-psychotics, and suffers from acute nightmares. For Sarah the descent into the cave may represent a more radical solution to the problem of how her grief can be healed, through a symbolic death of her old life and rebirth in the womb of the cave.

The idea may seem outlandish to modern readers, but has a mythic resonance highlighted by cultural theorist Mircea Eliade: 'The *return to origins* gives the hope of a rebirth ... [F]or archaic societies life cannot be *repaired*, it can only be re-created by a return to sources' (1964: 30). Jung too, in discussing forms of 'Rebirth' as one of his *Four Archetypes*, identifies one concerning:

> rebirth in the strict sense ... rebirth within the span of an individual life. [...] Rebirth may be renewal without any change of being, inasmuch as the personality which is renewed is not changed in its essential nature, but only its functions, or parts of the personality, are subjected to healing, strengthening, or improvement. Thus even bodily ills may be healed through rebirth ceremonies. (1986: 48)

The example he uses to illustrate this form of rebirth takes place, naturally, in a cave:

> The cave is the place of rebirth, that secret cavity in which one is shut up in order to be incubated and renewed ... Anyone who gets into that cave, that is to say into the cave which everyone has in himself, or into the darkness that lies behind consciousness, will find himself involved in an – at first – unconscious process of

transformation. By penetrating into the unconscious he makes a connection with his unconscious contents. (1986: 69-70)

Representations of the cave as womb have a long and distinguished heritage (see **Going Underground**), aligning the cave with the intrauterine qualities of other Terrible Places (the expression is Carol Clover's): the basements, sewers, underground lairs, mine shafts and tunnel systems where monsters dwell in horror films.

Freud, in his influential and endlessly re-interpreted essay 'The "Uncanny"', asserts that the womb is a quintessential generator of this eponymous sense. For Freud the 'uncanny is that class of the frightening which leads back to what is known of old and long familiar' (1955: 220) 'which has become alienated from it only through the process of repression' (1955: 241). Elsewhere he describes the womb as a paradigmatic example of 'what is known of old and long familiar', the source of us all:

It often happens that neurotic men declare that they feel there is something uncanny about the female genital organs. This unheimlich place, however, is the entrance to the former Heim [home] of all human beings, to the place where each of us lived once upon a time and in the beginning. There is a joking saying that 'Love is home-sickness'; and whenever a man dreams of a place or a country and says to himself, while he is still dreaming: 'this place is familiar to me, I've been here before,' we may interpret the place as being his mother's genitals or her body. (1955:245)

Freud's shift, later in the essay, to an exploration of castration anxiety as the key generative force behind the uncanny seems to sidestep the centrality of the womb, but critics exploring issues of gender and horror have returned it to centre stage.

Clover considers the Terrible Place of horror to contain a '"uterine" threat', the threat of dissolution, loss of self, reincorporation into the mother, that must be dispelled by the appropriation of phallic symbols, usually by a 'Final Girl' (see **Chicks with Picks**), 'in the service of sexual autonomy' (1992: 49) and delivery into the adult world.

Barbara Creed has written at greater length about womb anxiety in horror, asserting that for the dominant patriarchal culture woman's reproductive function renders her monstrous, although Creed acknowledges the lure of dissolution:

The archaic mother is present in all horror films as the blackness of extinction – death. The desires and fears invoked by the image of the archaic mother, as a force that threatens to reincorporate what it once gave birth to, are always there in the horror film ... The desire to return to the original oneness of things, to return to the mother/womb, is primarily a desire for non-differentiation. If ... life signifies discontinuity and separateness, and death signifies continuity and non-differentiation, then the desire for and attraction of death suggests also a desire to return to the state of original oneness with the mother. (1993: 28)

Creed here draws on the theories of Julia Kristeva, as expounded principally in *Powers of Horror*. According to Mary Ann Doane in *The Desire to Desire*, Kristeva:

associates the maternal with the abject – i.e., that which is the focus of a combined horror and fascination, hence subject to range of taboos designed to control the culturally marginal. In this analysis, the function of nostalgia for the mother-origin is that of a veil, a veil which conceals the terror attached to non-differentiation. The threat of the maternal space is that of the collapse of any distinction whatsoever between subject and object. (1987: 83)

Is this threat of reincorporation really enough to account for horror's insistent use of intrauterine imagery? Perhaps the womb represents death for us in ways other than a fear of or desire for non-differentiation: the sole certainty when we are born is that we will die; to be born is to be condemned to a certain death. The womb may represent, also, the only way we can imagine death; our non-existence is inconceivable, so we might imagine death to resemble a former period of 'unconscious' existence, our fetal development. Thinking about the womb further raises the fundamental, perhaps most uncomfortable metaphysical question: What happened to us before we were born? Where have we come from?

Yet something crucial is missing from these questions: an explicit sense of what a womb actually does. Neither Clover nor Creed pays much attention to the idea of birth, so we need to turn to one of Freud's contemporaries for a more compelling explanation of womb anxiety. Otto Rank, in *The Trauma of Birth*, originally published in 1924, argued that birth is not only the originary trauma of human experience, but also provides 'the ultimate biological basis of the psychical' (2010: xiii). For Rank the individual seeks throughout her life to return to the paradisial state of intrauterine existence, but the desire is repressed through the memory of this primal trauma, onto which all subsequent traumas are mapped.

Freud's enthusiasm for this idea wavered. Before the publication of Rank's book, in a footnote added to the second edition of *The Interpretation of Dreams*, Freud asserted that 'the act of birth is the first experience of anxiety, and thus the source and prototype of the affect of anxiety' (1959: 84). But following the publication of *The Trauma of Birth*, Freud dismissed Rank's idea that 'later attacks of anxiety were attempts at "abreacting" the trauma of birth' (1959: 86) by stating that while 'the act of birth, as the individual's first experience of anxiety, has given the affect of anxiety certain characteristic forms of expression' (1959: 93), 'I do not think that we are justified in assuming that wherever there is an outbreak of anxiety something like a reproduction of the situation of birth goes on in the mind' (1959: 94).

Tussles between Freud and Rank aside, how does *The Descent* relate to the birth process? While Rank distinguishes only between the paradisial existence in the womb and the traumatic exit from it, research psychiatrist Stanislav Grof, following Rank's lead, describes four stages, or 'Basic Perinatal Matrices' (BPMs), of the birth process and their psychical analogues. Grof's findings came from LSD research in the early to mid-1960s, and tend to support Rank's assertion that the birth process structures the unconscious. Grof's subjects often experienced the matrices sequentially; Sarah seems to follow a similar trajectory.

BPM I. Primal Union With the Mother (Intrauterine Experience Before the Onset of Delivery)

This stage represents the symbiotic relationship between mother and child, typified by a sense of oceanic calm, timelessness and joy. Such intrauterine experiences can however be disturbed by stress, disease, drug use and other physical disturbances.

The Descent's closest analogues to BPM I are the times when Sarah is happiest: white-water rafting at the beginning of the film, talking with her friends in the hut before the expedition, and during her hallucination of Jessica at the film's end. Clearly none of these represents the oceanic bliss of undisturbed intrauterine existence; even Sarah's happiest moments in the film are marked by flaws.

BPM II. Antagonism with the Mother (Contractions in a Closed Uterine System)

The first clinical stage of delivery: the uterus is contracting but the cervix is not yet open, creating a situation of emergency and threat. The psychic analogue to this experience is one of 'no exit' or hell, an intensely claustrophobic world characterised by darkness, despair and guilt. Grof notes that 'Typical physical symptoms associated with BPM II involve extreme pressures on the head and body ... excruciating pains in various parts of the body, difficulties with breathing, massive cardiac distress, and hot flushes and chills'. Symbolic analogues to this experience include 'the theme of descent into the underworld and the encounter with various monstrous entities', while real-life experiences recalling this matrix include 'injuries and accidents, excessive muscular exertion and exhaustion [and] experiences of imprisonment ... situations involving suffocation seem to be of special significance from this point of view' (1976: 121).

The key scenes representing BPM II in *The Descent* are those of the expedition moving through a series of tight, constricted passages, culminating in Sarah becoming trapped and the tunnel collapsing behind her. These scenes, before the crawlers have been seen, are often referred to by viewers as the most harrowing in the film; in the cast commentary of the British DVD release Marshall expresses surprise at the strength of people's responses to these scenes, which were explicitly designed to tap into people's claustrophobia.

They might work so well less by relating to a specific phobia than to the universal experience of birth. The situation for the cavers after the tunnel collapses is one of 'no exit', at least until the cave painting is discovered. The physical sensations listed by Grof as symptomatic of this matrix are recognisably those shown by Sarah while she is trapped in the tunnel, especially 'difficulty in breathing'. It's also worth noting that Grof describes guilt as an emotion symptomatic of this matrix. Sarah's struggle within the tunnel seems to be the catalyst for its collapse; indeed she nominated the tunnel as the way through in the first place, and guilt can be seen as a primary underlying motivation for her experiences (see **Nightmares in a Damaged Brain**).

BPM II is perhaps the paradigmatic horror space. Clover notes of the horror film's 'Terrible Tunnels' that they are 'dark, exitless, slick with blood and laced with heating ducts and plumbing pipes' (1992: 31). These first three qualities are so clearly intrauterine in nature as to need no further comment. The 'heating ducts and plumbing pipes' suggest a quality of interiority, of 'backstage', a paradigmatically uncanny quality of something that 'should be hidden but has come to light'. They also recall a modern tendency to regard the body as a machine, the result of the reification that is perhaps the natural result of an industrial approach to medicine, and common references to the genitourinary system as 'plumbing' or 'waterworks'.

Obviously narrow tunnels are to be found in both the natural and man-made worlds: squeezing through them does not necessarily mean that an individual is reliving the birth experience. So when is a tunnel just a tunnel? Not here: the film offers so many pointers towards an intrauterine interpretation that it would be churlish not to run with them.

BPM III. Synergism with the Mother (Propulsion through the Birth Canal)

The second clinical stage of delivery: the contractions continue but the cervix is open. The child is exposed to unbearable tension but there is at least the potential for release. Towards the end of this stage the child may be exposed to what has been termed 'abject' bodily matter: blood, mucus, urine, faeces. The psychic analogues to this situation are complex but tend to revolve around the confrontation with death. Grof lists the distinct experiential aspects of this matrix as 'titanic, sadomasochistic, sexual, and scatological' (1976: 124).

By 'titanic' Grof means a level of painful tension that reaches an inconceivable intensity, at which point it can become indistinguishable from an ecstatic rapture that takes delight in the extremes of violence to which the subject is being exposed: 'Subjects usually alternate experientially between the anxiety and suffering of the victim or victims and the ability to identify with the fury of the elemental forces and to enjoy the destructive energy' (1976: 125).

The sadomasochistic elements relate to the subject's ability to identify with individuals engaged in the most brutal kinds of violence:

they not only can understand the motivations of such deviants but that they themselves harbor in their unconscious forces of the same nature and intensity and could, under certain circumstances, commit similar crimes. They can assume quite readily all the roles involved in complex sadomasochistic scenes … (1976: 128)

Excessive sexual excitement can be felt but is ordinarily experienced by the entire body rather than solely the genital area. The scatological aspects derive from the child's exposure to the abject bodily wastes and a pleasure that can be taken in them.

If the sexual element of this matrix is absent in *The Descent*, the relevance of the other elements is clear. When the crawlers begin their attack Sarah, who has been until now distant, disconnected, panic-stricken, becomes fully alive and active. The savagery of her response to the crawlers' attacks is shocking: she buries a horn in the eye of one, and during her final fight alongside Juno she even bites one. She clearly takes pleasure in the violence, burying her thumbs deep in the eyes of a crawler long after it must have died. Elsewhere too her savagery and attitude to violence are ambivalent: she kills Beth, when her friend begs her to put her out of her misery, while her hobbling of Juno demonstrates the kind of ethical abdication associated by Grof with the sadomasochistic elements of this matrix. As with the 'titanic' experiences of Grof's subjects Sarah is both victim and perpetrator of violence, suffering herself and inflicting suffering on others.

The scatological elements are equally apparent in the film. Sarah falls into a pool of blood, from which she emerges only very slowly, as though delighted to feel herself surrounded by gore; afterwards she doesn't move while a crawler drools on her. When she encounters Juno later, her friend's shocked 'What happened to you?' refers at least as much to the grue sticking to Sarah's face and hair, which she has made no attempt to clean off, as to where she's been. Sarah's apparent pleasure in wallowing in waste is explained by Creed, for whom 'images of bodily wastes':

point back to a time when a 'fusion between mother and nature' existed; when bodily wastes, while set apart from the body, were not seen as objects of embarrassment and shame. Their presence in the horror film may invoke a response of disgust from the audience situated as it is within the social symbolic but at a more archaic level the representation of bodily wastes may invoke pleasure in breaking the taboo on filth –

sometimes described as a pleasure in perversity – and a pleasure in returning to that time when the mother-child relationship was marked by an untrammelled pleasure in 'playing' with the body and its wastes. (1993: 13)

BPM IV. Separation from the Mother (Termination of the Symbiotic Union and Formation of a New Type of Relationship)

The third clinical stage of delivery: the tension comes to an end, the child is delivered and takes its first breath, the cord connecting mother and child is cut, completing the physical separation from the mother. This matrix improves on the experience of the previous two but is less satisfactory than BPM I: the child's needs are no longer automatically met, and nor is it protected from the vicissitudes of the world; indeed it is extremely vulnerable. Psychic analogues with this matrix include the culmination of a physical, moral and spiritual crisis in the experience of ego death, followed by a sense of liberation and forgiveness. Symbolic analogues include the final victory over monsters, and escape from unendurable hardships.

In terms of *The Descent*, Sarah's climb up the mound of bones lit by a single ray of sunlight and her re-emergence into the world mark this matrix, although as we have noted previously this is a false delivery: 'really' she remains within the cave.

***

One of the appeals of this reading of the film is that it accounts for its otherwise uneven quality. A common complaint is that *The Descent*'s parts don't quite relate well enough to each other: that the first part, comprising the rafting scene, accident and hospital, is superfluous, or that the crawlers themselves are redundant in a film that makes such compelling use of its claustrophobically stifling tunnels. It has also been noted by some viewers that the constricted spaces and tight squeezes of the central part of the film are nowhere to be seen when the cavers encounter the crawlers; indeed the fights seem to take place in relatively wide, open spaces. These cease to be problems if we map Grof's sequence of BPMs onto what happens to Sarah, particularly the transition from BPMII to BPMIII, while the car crash itself provides the catalyst for this process of rebirth.

It's worth asking why, if we look at the film as an attempt to cure Sarah through a process of symbolic rebirth, this process fails. The most obvious answer, of course, is that she is a character in a horror film, a genre that – particularly in the 1970s heritage that the film pays tribute to – has an interest in downbeat endings.

We can also look for more local, story-specific explanations. Sarah has gone mad: the film is quite clear about this, even if the onset of her madness, or the relationship between her madness and the diegetic reality, and her ontological status itself, remain tantalisingly unclear. For Rank:

> In the meaning of this tendency to return to the mother, which the psychotic strives after by means of projection, the course of the psychotic disease, as Freud recognized, is actually to be interpreted as an attempt to cure ... Only the psychotic loses the way to the light of health in the labyrinth of the womb situation. (2010: 72)

A further explanation rests on Sarah's behaviour. A descent into savagery is necessary within the cave. Juno regresses to a state of instinctual violence, only to accidentally mortally wound Beth; yet she shows that she has retained a sense of civilised behaviour by insisting, against the wishes of the other survivors, that she wait for and attempt to rescue Sarah. Sarah's regression into savagery is marked, by contrast, by a deliberate wounding and abandonment of Juno. Where Juno goes back, selflessly, to try to save Sarah, Sarah's deliberate attack on Juno is entirely selfish and demonstrates that the bonds of civilisation have failed in her.

These bonds of civilisation are not synonymous with the social infrastructure that the expedition, in a sense, hopes to leave behind in the cave, but involve rather a fundamental recognition that we need each other, we rely on each other, a point made repeatedly and forcefully by other entries in what we might call 'endurance' cinema (see **Progeny**). That Sarah's mistreatment of Juno is key is stressed by the ghost of Juno appearing to Sarah in the SUV, which marks a final breakdown of narrative stability.

However necessary the cave is to our development, however crucial our need for the kind of death/rebirth attempted by Sarah, the cave, finally, must be transcended. The lessons learned in the cave must be applied outside it. Sarah's wilful embrace of the savagery of the cave, her abdication of human community in favour of vengeance, ensures that she remains lost in the labyrinth.

CHICKS WITH PICKS

I think as a couple of guys it was really important to us to get it as accurate as possible and not make it condescending to women or derogatory in any way. It had to be authentic. These were strong-willed independent contemporary women that we were trying to depict. We had to get it right. I, personally, as the writer, consulted a lot of women that I know just to get their feedback on it. Hopefully, it paid off. Neil Marshall in Guillen, 2006

Why should Marshall have chosen an all-female group for the film? Or rather: what difference does it make that it's all-female, rather than a mixture, or all-male? Marshall admits that his original concept for the film involved a mixed group, and that he was attracted to a colleague's off-hand suggestion of making the cavers an all-female group for its novelty. This takes us to the first, obvious point: it's a selling point, a distinguishing feature. As Marshall points out in 'The Making of *The Descent*', the film is unique among what Marshall describes as 'action horror' films in having an all-female cast.

Given that the cast is all-female – and young, athletic and attractive to boot – Marshall's treatment of them is remarkably desexualised, arguably working against this selling point, for at least some of the film's audience. With the possible exception of some shots of Juno in her partially unzipped lycra top, there is very little in the way of titillation in the film. Not that the film lacks opportunities: we see Rebecca in the shower, for instance, and flashback sex scenes between Paul and Sarah, or indeed Paul and Juno, wouldn't have looked too out of place. Even the crawlers could have been portrayed as presenting a sexual threat, as their counterparts do in *The Cavern*. This lack of sexual interest aligns *The Descent* squarely with Marshall's other films. But the decision to present the women neutrally – not only desexualised but also, perhaps, defeminised – also relates to the underlying themes in the film.

None of the women is married. None has children – Sarah, of course, had both a husband and a child but they are now dead. Sarah seems to have been more attached to her child than to her husband – the name on her lips when she wakes up in hospital is 'Jessie' and her hallucinations invariably feature her daughter rather than Paul. Juno is sexualised insofar as we suspect she has had an affair with Paul; if anything she seems more upset by his death than Sarah does, carrying a memento with her in the shape of a pendant around her neck marked with what was evidently Paul's catchphrase: 'Love each day'. Sam refers to her boyfriend, who gave her the watch that prompts howls of derision from Holly; in one of the deleted scenes Sam shows Holly a picture of him. The decision to leave this photo out of the finished film means that Paul is not only its sole male character but essentially the only human male seen on-screen, and his appearance is so brief that it amounts to little more than a narrative convenience. The absence of sexual flashbacks, or indeed any indication of real passion within the Sarah-Paul-Juno triangle reinforces this sense that Paul is simply a narrative marker.

The others are given no history of partners. Holly is a self-confessed 'sports fuck', with no time for men, although she plans to have 'loads of babies' when she's older; Rebecca seems too hung up on health and safety to have sex; and Beth, the only character whose job is mentioned in the film, is similarly unattached.

Although the women are thus broadly desexualised, both in terms of presentation and narrative, there are sexual stress points within the group; indeed the absence of men creates a kind of vacuum increasing the tension among the characters. Sarah and Juno, who are along with Sam portrayed as securely heterosexual, orbit around the memory of Paul, while there are subtle hints that Holly and Beth may be lesbian. The two are depicted as being at odds from the outset, with Beth muttering 'Here we go' as Holly introduces herself to the group in the hut, as though there were some unspoken conflict or competition between them – a recognition in each other, perhaps, of a desire that is, in terms of the group dynamic and its long-held friendships, illicit. Holly is overtly 'sporty', with her spiky hair and penchant for base jumping; she is the 'protégé', a suggestive term, of fellow 'sports fuck' Juno, and she reacts violently when Juno touches her after the cave-in, as though overly sensitive about being touched by other women.

Beth's coding is perhaps more direct: she is older than the others, at twenty-five, and an English teacher. She is sensible, level-headed and extremely protective of Sarah, with whom she has a close bond. It is Beth who calms Sarah down in the hospital; Beth who tells Holly to 'fuck off' after Sarah's encounter with the bats; Beth who helps Sarah when she is stuck in the tunnel. But it is also Beth who tells Sarah that Juno fatally wounded her, intimating that it was a deliberate act on her part and aligning it with Juno's affair with Paul. Why should Beth think that Juno has deliberately wounded her? It is clearly, to us, an accident. Does Beth resent Juno's influence over Sarah – is she jealous of Juno, jealous enough to turn Sarah against her?

These signals are subtle, but add to the tension within the group; they also help to represent Holly and Beth as problematic characters. Holly's gung-ho attitude ensures that she bullishly pushes ahead, deaf to Juno's pleading that she slow down, until she injures herself, endangering the group; it is also her desire for something tougher than a 'tourist trap' like Boreham Caverns that drives Juno's decision to opt for an unexplored system. Juno wants Holly to be impressed, and can't resist smiling when Holly says that the cave isn't as dull as she'd expected. Beth too, as we have seen, misinterprets Juno's attack, which obviously puts Juno in danger and arguably endangers Sarah too, isolating her with only her splintered mind for company.

Whether any members of the party are lesbian or not, they all clearly follow non-traditional gender roles: none, as we have noted, has a husband or a child, and they are engaged in an extreme sports activity more often associated with men. In a sense they have rejected a kind of normative femininity in a bid to usurp a traditionally masculine realm. Their clothes, while entirely credible in the context of their environment, erase any signs of sexual difference, lending them what Barbara Creed terms fully symbolic bodies, bearing 'no indication of [their] debt to nature' (1993: 11). For theorists such as Julia Kristeva the female body is more ordinarily associated with nature than culture: Yet throughout the film the illusion of the fully symbolic body becomes untenable, as limbs snap and characters wallow in blood. Their bodies' 'debt to nature' becomes all too apparent, returning them to what Kristeva would perhaps consider a more authentic association: 'the image of woman's body, because of its maternal functions, acknowledges its "debt to nature" and consequently is more likely to signify the abject' (Creed 1993: 11). This trajectory marks a shift between what Creed describes as 'the law of the father' and 'the maternal authority' (1993: 13), with the latter finally proving dominant.

This idea of the law of the father deserves greater attention, even if it takes us into murky psychoanalytic waters. In their bid to reject the 'maternal authority' the expedition members attempt to usurp this law, characteristically associated in psychoanalytic theory with the emergence into the symbolic realm and the related acquisition of language, along with the authority to confer names. Juno leaves the guidebook to Boreham

Caverns behind, perhaps marking a rejection of pre-existing language; she wants them to discover and name a new, unexplored system. Beth's job here, as English teacher, is noteworthy: she has taken what is in psychoanalytic terms a masculine role, in a job related to the acquisition and use of language. The crawlers, by contrast, appear to have no language, marking them as entirely outside the symbolic realm.

In other ways the cavers seem eminently capable of filling 'masculine' roles: they are tough and independent, but also realistically depicted, a point highlighted by Beth's statement, on seeing the entrance to the cave, that 'I'm an English teacher, not fucking Tomb Raider'. They fight bravely, and put themselves willingly through gruelling feats of endurance for the good of the group. Contrary to genre expectations, moreover, there's no rescue mounted by a square-jawed sheriff, or by Sam's boyfriend, alarmed at how long they've been in the cave. The women are left to fend for themselves, and acquit themselves admirably, for all that the odds are stacked against them.

Yet there are indications throughout that the gender politics of a film that might on the surface seem to valorise female autonomy and independence actually revolves around an implicit reinforcement of traditional gender roles. Take the naming of the cave, for instance. There is a suggestion that Juno's desire to name the cave relates to her continued attachment to Paul: she suggests to Sarah that the cave system could be named after her, presumably meaning her married name, and thus Paul's.

Such jockeying for position around an absent male is evident also in the relays of pendant possession. The pendant is a phallic object which has been put into circulation by the film's sole male character as a mark of his approval. Possession of it confers power – a power marked as phallic, in contrast to, for instance, the ring Sarah would have received from Paul as his wife. Initially worn by Juno, the indisputable leader of the pack, the pendant is torn from her neck by Beth, who clutches it in what appear to be her death throes. But the pendant – or possession of the phallus, in psychoanalytic terms – is too powerful to allow her to die; she must give it to Sarah first. Sarah's possession of the pendant ensures in turn that she will survive.

Elsewhere the cavers appear to explore their autonomy only by acting like men, calling each other 'guys' and arguing over levels of technical proficiency. This is not to suggest some form of essentialised femininity to which the characters should adhere; rather that within the film this itself appears as an implicit suggestion. The cavers have no families, no ties, unlike the crawlers. All of the crawlers that we see except one are male, suggesting that while the males hunt, the females tend the young. The only female crawler we see appears after a child crawler attacks Sarah, reminding the viewer (and, perhaps, Sarah) of the traditional gender roles they have abandoned.

Within the context of the film, are the cavers being punished for their abandonment of traditional gender roles? We probably wouldn't ask the question of an all-male cast: are the characters in *Dog Soldiers* being punished, and if so for what? Machismo? Fear of women? It's tempting, though, given the nature of what happens to the women here, to answer this question in the affirmative: they attempt to usurp the traditionally masculine domains of exploration and language, and find themselves in an intrauterine space that threatens to eat them up – the feminine repressed, that is, returning with a vengeance.

In 'The Making of *The Descent*' cast and crew members are asked what scares them. Marshall jokingly repeats Cooper's (Kevin McKidd) answer to the same question in *Dog Soldiers*: 'Spiders ... women. Spider women.' This points to a persistent feature in the depiction of women in Marshall's films: as a rule, they are not to be trusted. The films show an ambivalent attitude towards femininity: his female characters are strong, insofar, like Juno here or Sinclair (Rhona Mitra) in *Doomsday* (2008), as they are warlike. But they are also untrustworthy: Megan (Emma Cleasby) in *Dog Soldiers* betrays the platoon of soldiers who have trusted her with their lives; a woman picked up off the streets of a post-apocalyptic Glasgow in *Doomsday* slits the throats of her would-be rescuers; and Etain (Olga Kurylenko) betrays the Ninth Legion in *Centurion* (2010) by leading them into an ambush. Here Juno, who may already have betrayed Sarah by sleeping with her husband, betrays the group by lying to them about the cave system they are about to explore; and Sarah not only betrays Juno by wounding her but demonstrates that her subjectivity itself is untrustworthy. The film allows her narrative centrality, her viewpoint dominant throughout the film, only to disallow it on the grounds that it cannot be trusted, resurrecting an age-old association between woman and madness that often delimits the trustworthiness of female subjectivity (see **Nightmares in a Damaged Brain**).

The Descent's feminist credentials have been challenged by a number of critics along similar lines. For *Slant Magazine*'s Ed Gonzalez: 'The darkness inside the cave makes sense but it's politically reductive: Marshall fails to create compelling women distinguishable from one another ... These women primarily exist as sheep being led to the slaughter' (2006). *The Ruthless Reviews* reviewer suggests, only half-jokingly, that 'the story becomes a repudiation of feminism, as it argues that women are their own worst enemies, and because they are disloyal, adulterous, and back-stabbing, it's best that they kill each other and let men take care of their own interests' (Cale, 2006). And according to Lisa Morton's *Throwdown* Review the film's message is that 'women really don't belong out in the wilds, and can't rely on each other when things go wrong. The closest thing the movie has to a plot turn in its latter half centers on a betrayal, so once again the message seems to be that women are inherently catty and vicious' (2005).

That, at any rate, is one way of interpreting the film. *The Descent*'s persistent use of quotations, images lifted wholesale from other films, suggests another. Towards the end of the film Sarah is spattered with blood and wide-eyed with craziness, in a sequence of shots that recalls Sally from *The Texas Chain Saw Massacre* (Tobe Hooper, 1974) and the eponymous *Carrie* (Brian De Palma, 1976).

Like Carrie and Sally, Sarah has been driven insane by her ordeal; like them she is both victim and hero. Horror films tend towards not only a thematic cannibalism but a perpetual reuse of specific images, often simply marking a lack of imagination on the part of the filmmakers. *The Descent*'s use of quotations seems more measured and focused, in the service of misdirection (the *Deliverance* quotations near the start of the film might lead us to expect a hillbilly showdown) or, as here, a kind of semiotic playfulness.

The Descent, in this light, appears less a film about women stuck in a cave than a film about the representation of women in horror. For Mark Bernard, in *Selling the Splat Pack: the DVD Revolution and the American Horror Film*, 'The representations of monstrous women in ... Marshall's film draw so heavily and overtly from images of monstrous women from past horror films that [they] seem to interrogate, rather than substantiate, the idea of woman-as-monstrous' (2010: 228).

*Blood-spattered female protagonists (from top): Sarah (*The Descent*), the eponymous Carrie and Sally in* The Texas Chain Saw Massacre

The film draws attention to its own process of production not only through quoting other films but also through its use of Holly's DV camera. This is, of course, a quotation of its own, aligning the film with the vérité scenes from *Cannibal Holocaust* (Ruggero Deodato, 1980) and *The Blair Witch Project* (Daniel Myrick, Eduardo Sánchez, 1999) among others; but its use here serves perhaps less to bolster the film's sense of authenticity than to remind us that we are watching a film. The most telling sequence in this respect comes when Sarah wakes up after the first crawler attack. We see her first through the display panel of the DV camera, a peculiar shot because there is nobody present (apart, of course, from us) to look through the display; usually DV or cine camera footage within a film presupposes the presence of *someone filming*. Shortly afterwards Sarah is unable to stop watching through the camera as Holly's body is eaten, even though the sight makes her retch, endangering her life by alerting the crawlers to her presence, and she could easily close the display, or simply stop watching. Yet Sarah is, like the viewers of the film, compelled to watch; both she and we have a compulsive urge to see just how bad it can get.

For Bernard this reflexivity demonstrates how we should interpret the characters' behaviour:

> evaluating *The Descent* as intertextual and metacinematic helps to retain the film's capacity for a progressive political reading while not eliding the problematic connections that that film and our patriarchal culture make between femininity and monstrousness. In *The Descent*, the female characters appear and act monstrous because patriarchy, as represented by the Crawlers, forces them to, just as patriarchal culture has often constructed femininity as monstrous and has rarely been able to understand and represent women's desire as anything other than horrifying. Marshall's radical bricolage in *The Descent* foregrounds the constructedness of representation and allows the spectator to notice these constructions and, perhaps, question them. (2010: 250-251)

The Descent's intertextual references go beyond citing other films; the portrayal of the women here, particularly Sarah, seems almost a dialogue with or riposte to academic studies of gender in horror, most notably Carol Clover's highly influential *Men, Women and Chainsaws*.

Clover argues that horror tends to draw on a premodern notion of 'one-sex reasoning', in which 'the body with its one elastic sex was far freer to express theatrical gender and the anxieties thereby produced than it would be when it came to be regarded as the foundation of gender' (Lacquer in Clover, 1992: 16). In this world sex proceeds from gender: '[a] figure does not cry and cower because she is a woman; she is a woman because she cries and cowers' (1992: 13), and 'there is something about the victim function that wants manifestation in a female' (1992: 12).

Clover cites Jurij Lotman's description of the two subject functions or positions in myth – 'a mobile, heroic being who crosses boundaries and penetrates closed spaces, and an immobile being who personifies that damp, dark space and constitutes that which is to be overcome' (Clover 1992: 13) – and notes that the first function is inescapably coded male, and the second female. By this token, then, the cavers in *The Descent*, whatever their visible gender, are male; their apparent rejection of normative femininity is less a lifestyle choice than a consequence of their narrative function. *The Descent* playfully inverts Lotman's narrative positions – the female cavers perform a male function while the predominantly male crawlers perform a female function – but keeps this from being a schematic inversion by muddying the waters. Sarah has indulged in the uniquely female activity of childbirth, and the male crawlers are encountered in the profoundly feminine realm of the cave system. These are also relatively credible characters, rather than simple expressions of narrative positions or functions; any sense of an allegorical or symbolic meaning can be balanced out by a recognition that the essential set-up of *The Descent* – a group of women goes caving – is far from unbelievable. This is not to say that the film cannot be interpreted according to Clover's model; rather that it is aware of its genre heritage, especially relating to issues of gender, and adopts a playful, reflexive tone to these issues.

Victims in horror films, as has often been noted, tend to be female, with male victims more commonly found in action films revolving around suspense rather than horror's characteristic shock and disgust. Yet for Clover part of the pleasure of watching horror films comes from a play with gender, a structural ambiguity:

> I have argued against the temptation to read the body in question as 'really' male (masquerading as female) or 'really' female (masquerading as male), suggesting instead

that the excitement is precisely predicated on the undecidability or both-andness or one-sexedness of the construction'. (1992: 217)

This 'undecidability' is for Clover embodied in the figure of the Final Girl, like Sally in *The Texas Chain Saw Massacre* and Sarah in *The Descent*: victim, hero and central character. For Clover the Final Girl is:

The one character of stature who does live to tell the tale ... She is introduced at the beginning and is the only character to be developed in any psychological detail. We understand immediately from the attention paid it that hers is the main story line. She is intelligent, watchful, levelheaded; the first character to sense something amiss and the only one to deduce from the accumulating evidence the pattern and extent of the threat; the only one, in other words, whose perspective approaches our own privileged understanding of the situation. (1992: 44)

From this account Sarah 'fits', albeit imperfectly: she may be the first person to see the crawlers, and she is the only known survivor, but she is anything but levelheaded, becoming hysterical on encountering the bats and a tunnel she cannot quite squeeze through, nominating the tunnel that collapses behind her and leading the expedition directly into a crawler attack. Clover even anticipates Sarah's fate by describing the potential for a female slide from victim to hero to go too far, leading a character 'into the sort of hypermasculinity that fares so badly in horror' (1992: 107).

Yet why, Clover asks, should there be a Final Girl at all? As horror audiences can identify across gender, what is to be gained by running fantasies of victimhood through female characters? Clover submits that 'there is the female body itself, the metaphoric architecture of which, with its enterable but unseeable inner space, has for so long been a fixture in the production of the uncanny' and, more importantly, that 'the use of woman [is] a kind of feint, a front through which the boy can simultaneously experience forbidden desires and disavow them on grounds that the visible actor is, after all, a girl' (1992: 18).

What kind of 'forbidden desires' might be repressed in watching *The Descent*? Clover argues that in general horror's use of female victims serves to obscure a male drive towards a masochism coded as feminine. She explains that for Freud, 'although masochism "is a centrally structuring element in both male and female subjectivity", it is only in the female that it is accepted and natural and thus only in the male that it is considered perverse or pathological' (1992: 214).

Why should masochism be considered perverse for men? Clover further explicates Freud: 'all children, male and female, are subject to the unconscious fantasy that they are being beaten – that is, "loved" – by the *father*. Whereas the girl's fantasy is "straight" (at least in Freud's reading), the boy's involves a gender complication: to be beaten/loved by his father requires the adoption of a position coded as "feminine" or receptively homosexual' (1992: 214). For Clover masochism, rather than sadism, is the chief structuring principle of horror, a 'feminine masochism' which, when experienced and enjoyed by male viewers, can be disavowed on the grounds that the visible subject is female.

I would take this model of a gender-related feint or displacement further for The Descent. The film is structured to play like an exploration of gender roles for women and the return of the feminine repressed. Yet the key theme mobilised in the film, that of birth anxiety, is one that belongs or applies to both men and women. Its appearance here, in a film populated only by women, might make the viewer think that all that messy business about wombs and intrauterine tunnels is an exclusively feminine concern. It isn't, as can be seen not least from the fact that the film is effective across the gender divide; but running it through female characters makes it more 'allowable'. What Otto Rank would term the repressed desire to relive the originary trauma can be disavowed on the grounds that the visible actors here are women.

NIGHTMARES IN A DAMAGED BRAIN

What it is about is a descent into madness. Neil Marshall, 'The Making of *The Descent*'

Fan responses to *The Descent* have tended to stress the point that Sarah is hallucinating by the end of the film, and to ask precisely when these hallucinations begin. According to Marshall, Sarah's hallucinations begin when she wakes up in the lair after injuring Juno and falling down a tunnel.

Sarah wakes up in the bone-strewn lair …

When she awakens, surrounded by bones, she can see daylight – not a diegetic impossibility, because their earlier visit to the lair might have been at night, although Juno has earlier pointed out when Holly believes she has seen daylight that they are two miles underground – and climbs a mound of bones to emerge through the ground. She runs to the jeep – some viewers have suggested that the fact she finds it so easily indicates this must be a fantasy; conversely it could simply be cinematic shorthand – and drives back onto the main road, only to be jolted out of her fantasy and returned to the cave, where she begins another fantasy, of being with her daughter.

Marshall describes her second awakening in the lair as happening in exactly the same place as the first, thereby demonstrating that her escape was a discrete fantasy; but when she awakens the second time there are no bones in view.

… or does she?

The entire sequence is, in fact, profoundly destabilising and raises more questions than it answers; it's worth breaking it down into its constituent parts.

After Sarah sees a ghostly Juno in the SUV with her, the film cuts to a shot of her screaming. In this shot, near-subliminal in length, she is not clearly shown as being in the SUV.

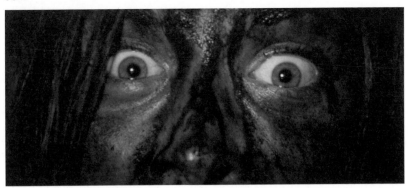

Wide-eyed with craziness

When she 'awakens' once more, she can see Jessica sitting beyond a birthday cake, facing her.

Happy Birthday Jessica

The film then cuts to an image of Sarah gazing into empty space beyond her still-burning torch, and pulls back to reveal that she is in some kind of hollow on a cliff, with the sounds of the crawlers all around her.

Alone in the cave

Are we to take this final scene as 'real'? She appeared earlier to fall down to the bone-strewn lair; she no longer seems to be there, and there is no indication of how she might have arrived at this hollow. Indeed the scene has such a nightmarish quality, with Sarah dwarfed by the immensity of the cave around her, that it is tempting to see it as yet another level of her hallucination.

If it is unclear where Sarah's hallucinations end, it is equally unclear where they begin. The ending is so unstable that it casts a shadow over everything we have seen before; by now our reality-testing capacity has been so sorely tried and undermined that we can easily imagine that Sarah's hallucinations begin much earlier.

So what are the possible entry points to Sarah's private reality? Do her hallucinations begin as a result of claustrophobia induced by being trapped in the tunnel? On entering the cave? At the point of being panicked by the bats? This last would at least account for the batlike qualities of the crawlers. Or perhaps her hallucinations begin earlier: when she awakens from her dream in the hut – there is, notably, no start to this dream; the film simply cuts into it – has she fallen into another, more elaborate dream? It's worth enumerating the points at which Sarah awakens, as each could mark a possible rift with consensus reality: at the hospital, at the hut, on emerging from the collapsed tunnel, after the initial crawler attack, and after wounding Juno and falling down a hole (twice).

Even within the diegesis she is, of course, seen to hallucinate, or dream: once at the hospital, where she is chased by darkness down a corridor, and later during her dream at the hut. While the former has an unrealistic, expressionist feel, the latter is indistinguishable from the diegetic reality: in her dream she believes that she is awake in the hut, where she 'really' went to sleep, conjuring the nightmare image of the nested worlds of sleep paralysis. Only her awakening from it (forced, perhaps, by the shock of taking a length of pipe in the eye) demonstrates to us that this was a dream. If Sarah never 'woke up', we would have no way – other, perhaps, than even more acute demands on our reality testing, which might simply lead us to consider the film poorly made – to distinguish Sarah's subjective experience from the film's diegetic reality.

The two are inseparable, in any case. While Sarah is not the sole viewpoint character of the film – there are scenes in which she does not appear, particularly during the hut sequence, which perhaps favours Juno more, and during the fight with the crawlers – she is by some margin its most privileged figure. We are exposed to her subjective fantasies, as we are not to those of the other characters, and she is, or at least appears to be, the sole survivor.

She is also the central character with respect to the events of the film: it is the loss of her husband and child, rather than that of Juno's lover, with which we are encouraged to sympathise, and the expedition seems to have been arranged specifically for her. She also drives the action, nominating the tunnel that takes them deeper into the cave complex, prompting its collapse and seeing the crawlers before anyone else: the film's narrative is very much about what happens to Sarah.

Not only do we experience her subjective reality; we are also reminded several times of the possibility that she might hallucinate. She is on medication, as we see in the hut, but has left her pills behind for the caving expedition; and as they approach the cave entrance Rebecca regales the cavers with a list of the things that might happen to them in the dark: 'You can get dehydration, disorientation, claustrophobia, panic attacks, paranoia, hallucinations, visual and aural ...' Sarah is jumpy as soon as they arrive in the cave, panicking when caught in a flight of bats, and the others' awareness of her heightened sensitivity means they reject her initial sighting of a crawler as a hallucination.

And indeed much of the film does have a profoundly hallucinatory quality. If we view Sarah's journey through the prism of Grof's BPM matrices, it follows a trajectory more commonly seen in LSD experiments than run-of-the-mill caving expeditions, while the use of differently coloured lights to distinguish one character from another when they are split up in the cave bathes the film's events in an unrealistic, numinous glow.

The film's themes also tend towards a sense that this is some kind of interior phantasy, particularly the idea of guilt, which characterises Sarah's actions almost from the beginning of the film. Immediately before Paul crashes into the oncoming van he turns to face Sarah, taking his eyes off the road, his attention distracted by her asking him if everything's OK. We can assume that Sarah suffers from survivor guilt: the nightmare she has in the hut shows her suffering a similar fate to her husband and (presumably) daughter.

When Sarah enters the cave she goes on to endanger herself and her friends: apart from nominating the tunnel which collapses after she has become trapped in it, she later tells Juno to throw away a flare, in the belief that light will attract the crawlers; in fact they are blind and the loss of light serves only to disorient the women. When they find themselves in the crawlers' lair, Sarah's 'This way!' leads them directly into an attack.

Later she kills a child crawler, echoing her own guilt over the death of her daughter and inviting an attack from a vengeful crawler mother. Guilt, finally, follows her treatment of Juno at the end; after her 'escape', Juno, pallid and ghostly, appears in the SUV beside her, a vision which prompts a retreat into the relatively comforting hallucination of her daughter.

Related to this sense of guilt are indications within the film that Sarah should be identified with the crawlers, and not only from the severity of her violence: towards the end she screams, but the others hear only a crawler scream; when she picks herself up from the ground on her final awakening in the lair she moves like a crawler; and her vomit when she leans out of the jeep towards the end of the film looks much like the crawlers' drool. *

Moving like a crawler

This sense that attacker and attacked represent the same person is one familiar to us through nightmares; as Clover argues: 'We are both Red Riding Hood and the Wolf; the force of the experience, in horror, comes from "knowing" both sides of the story' (1992: 12).

The cave itself also has hallucinatory qualities. The experience of entering a cave might be neurologically hardwired for humans as the threshold of a hallucinatory state. The entrance into what is known as 'Stage 3' hallucinatory imagery is characterised for many people by:

a swirling vortex or rotating tunnel that seems to surround them and to draw them into its depths ... Westerners use culture-specific words like 'funnels, alleys, cones, vessels, pits [and] corridors' to describe the vortex. In other cultures, it is often experienced as entering a hole in the ground. Shamans typically speak of reaching the spirit world via such a hole. (Lewis-Williams 2002: 128-9)

Shamanic peoples, those who have most successfully integrated hallucinatory experiences into their cultures, often refer to the extreme violence experienced in the visionary state. Lewis-Williams cites D. Whitley as listing death/killing, aggression/fighting, drowning/going underwater and bodily transformation as part of a 'shamanistic symbolic repertoire' (2002: 173) in North America. Lewis-Williams goes on to suggest that: 'An association of fighting with North American shamans is ... suggested by the Yokuts term *tsesas* which means spirit helper, shaman's talisman, and stone knife. Moreover, among some south-central California groups the words for *shaman*, *grizzly bear*, and *murderer* were interchangeable' (2002: 174).

Once in 'Stage 3' proper, people tend to forget they are hallucinating: 'Subjects stop using similes to describe their experiences and assert that the images are indeed what they appear to be. They "lose insight into the differences between literal and analogical meanings"' (Lewis-Williams 2002: 16). Hallucinations of this kind can, then, be intensely violent and are indistinguishable from consensus reality.

The cave painting also hints at a hallucinatory nature to Sarah's experiences. For Lewis-Williams such paintings fix hallucinatory images in physical space:

in these subterranean images, we have an ancient and unusually explicit expression of a complex shamanistic experience that was given its form by altered states of consciousness. That experience comprised isolation from other people, sensory deprivation by entrance into the underground realm, possible ingestion of psychotropic substances, 'death' by a painful ordeal of multiple piercing, and emergence from those dark regions into the light. (2002: 282)

We might even see the film's iconography of holes in heads as indicating that it relates to inner experience: following Paul's pole through the skull we see Sarah suffering a similar fate during her dream at the hut, while crawlers are variously dispatched with a pick to the top of the head, a tusk in the eye and two thumbs buried deep in their eye sockets.

It's worth mentioning that despite the hallucinatory, low-mythic qualities of Sarah's experiences, any sense of transcendence is absent. Unlike, say, the white-faced ghouls of *Carnival of Souls* (Herk Harvey, 1962), which crowd around Mary Henry (Candace Hilligross) in an apparent attempt to make her realise something, the crawlers are broadly realistic. They may be hallucinations, but they are not demonic, or supernatural – they can be killed, or wounded.

This is especially noteworthy given Sarah's situation. Carol Clover suggests that:

> The 'recent loss' trope is so standard as to be a virtual sine qua non of supernatural horror. Usually it is the death or divorce-departure of a parent ... but it may also be the loss of a child ... or the loss of a spouse or lover ... In this way, as in others, supernatural horror is like the European fairy tale, which frequently takes as its point of departure the death of someone near (usually a parent). In the case of horror, the point seems to be that such a loss opens a space for the supernatural, and that immediate survivors are 'open' to otherworldly invasion. (1992: 73)

The Descent looks like a supernatural horror film, mobilising associations of caves with the underworld through its red flares and the seemingly endless trials suffered by the cavers. Even the womb imagery of the film is more traditionally associated with the supernatural. For Clover such imagery is almost only found in horror in supernatural stories:

> The importance of reproductive themes and images to Satanic/possession stories emerges clearly in the comparison with other brands of horror, in which they are by and large absent. Sex, in a variety of forms, looms large in the thematic "field" of the standard slasher, vampire, werewolf, zombie, and even rape-revenge film, but reproduction, when it occurs at all, occurs only in passing ... It is the possession film – stories that hinge on psychic breaking and entering – that plunges us repeatedly into a world of menstruation, pregnancy, fetuses, abortion, miscarriage, amniotic fluid, childbirth, breastfeeding. (1992: 82)

These suggestions are in a sense one more red herring on Marshall's part. In line with Marshall's other films, there is no sense of the sacred, or of God here. *The Descent*'s metaphysics are delimited by the human, the material: any 'other worlds' it explores are expressions of psychosis and interiority rather than revelation or gnosis. This aligns Marshall with what we might call a modernist approach to fantasy, in which explanations for the fantastic have been displaced from the supernatural realm to that of psychology.

Rosemary Jackson charts this shift in her study *Fantasy*:

Fantasy shifts from one 'explanation' of otherness to another in the course of its history. It moves from supernaturalism and magic to theology and science to categorize or define otherness. Freud's theories of the Unconscious are one means of explaining, or rationalizing, this realm. (1981: 158)

It needn't be this way. Horror is one of the few genres where transcendence is still an option in an avowedly materialist culture. Indeed, as Victoria Nelson has argued in *The Secret Life of Puppets*, the materialist suppression of the possibility of transcendence, of another realm, may be a structural factor underpinning supernatural horror:

our culture's post-Reformation, post-Enlightenment prohibition on the supernatural and exclusion of a transcendent, nonmaterialist level of reality from the allowable universe has created the ontological equivalent of a perversion caused by repression. Lacking an allowable connection with the transcendent, we have substituted an obsessive, unconscious focus on the negative dimension of the denied experience ... But as Paul Tillich profoundly remarked, 'Wherever the demonic appears, there the question of its correlate, the divine, will also be raised'. (2001: 19)

The absence of the demonic, the supernatural, from *The Descent*, makes any kind of divine rescue, or purpose, impossible; and this lack of transcendence, this refusal to entertain the possibility of the supernatural, contributes in no small part to the bleakness of the film.

Some viewers have suggested that Sarah is killed in the car crash that opens the film, and that the events of the film depict her attempt to come to terms with what has happened to her. The belief that people who have suffered violent, unexpected deaths do not realise that they are dead is popular in many cultures. Even people who have died more placid deaths are said by some not to go directly to their final destination:

first they have to undergo a series of unusual adventures, ordeals and trials. Sometimes these adventures involve travelling through dangerous landscapes not dissimilar to earthly deserts, high mountains, jungles or swamps. The soul may have to encounter and combat various strange beings and fantastic creatures. (Grof 1980: 16)

The trope of the victim of violent death who does not realise they are dead is also popular in horror films, informing not only cult favourites like *Carnival of Souls* and *Dead End* (Jean-Baptiste Andrea, 2003) but also big-budget, major studio outings like *Jacob's Ladder* (Adrian Lyne, 1990) and *The Sixth Sense* (M. Night Shyamalan, 1999).

All of these films, however, have a coda or climax that shows viewers that the characters they have been watching are already dead. At the end of *Carnival of Souls* Mary Henry's car is dredged out of a river, containing her corpse and demonstrating that she has died in the accident witnessed at the beginning of the film. The eponymous *Dead End* proves to be a car crash with no survivors, but to the occupants of the car even a series of bizarre, inexplicable events cannot jolt them out of their conviction that they are still on their way to see an ageing family member for Christmas. In *Jacob's Ladder* a US soldier in Vietnam is suffering not only from a fatal war wound but also from government-sponsored chemical experimentation that makes him hallucinate being Macauley Culkin's father, amongst others horrors. In *The Sixth Sense* Malcolm Crowe (Bruce Willis) realises that when Cole Sear (Haley Joel Osment) says 'I see dead people' he's not kidding, an altercation early in the film having resulted in Crowe's death, of which he is unaware.

The Descent shares the idea of sudden death – another car crash – with these films but offers us no dependable vision of an objective reality beyond Sarah's subjective realities, nested inside each other like Russian dolls. The film does however contain enough hints to make the idea that she is already dead a tantalising suggestion.

When Sarah wakes up in the hospital bed she pulls out her various medical tubes, making her heart monitor flatline. In her dream in the hut, a pole crashes through the window and spears Sarah's skull through her eye: is this a reference to what has 'actually' happened, her death in the accident that killed her husband and child?

Several viewers have commented that the entrance to the cave resembles a grave, while descending into a cave has parallels with the commonly reported tunnels or vortices of Near Death Experiences (NDEs).

Looking into their own grave

The image of bats circling around the entrance to the cave, seen from within, recalls Hieronymous Bosch's painting of *The Ascent into the Empyrean*, while the cave's two entrances align it with the double portals of several mythical caves:

> The Mithraem, like Homer's Cave of the naiad nymphs ... has two entrances, one for mortals, one for the immortals, as Homer says. According to Mithraism, the two entrances are for souls descending into the sensible world ... and for immortal souls re-ascending. (Weinberg 1986: 151)

Light at the end?

But suggesting that Sarah is already dead, and that the events of the film represent some kind of dying fantasy, does not foreclose on other interpretations: that she is alive and hallucinating, or that she is 'really' being attacked by monsters. The film refuses to commit itself to a clear, obvious interpretation of events, allowing the viewer to entertain several interpretations simultaneously. The ambiguity only adds to the richness of the film, and its pleasure for the viewer, its undecidability.

But this ambiguity has a limit. Within the film it is clear by the end that if Sarah is not dead she has gone mad; the question concerning her madness is more 'when did it start?' than 'is she/isn't she?' The fact that we cannot know when Sarah's madness starts for sure, that it is impossible wholly to extricate a sense of 'objective' reality from Sarah's subjectivity, points to two factors: the peculiarity of cinema's elision of subjective and objective viewpoints, and the tendency of modern narratives to cohere around specific individuals.

Film has no way, unlike the written word, of clearly marking shifts from broadly subjective, viewpointed imagery to 'objective', diegetic realities, although such shifts happen innumerable times through most feature films. Broad shifts between the two are generally understood, even if only implicitly, by cine-literate viewers used to idiosyncrasies of soundtrack, acting, editing, camera placement and (more rarely) image distortion or the kinds of expressionist sets used in films explicitly about madness, such as *Das Kabinett des Doktor Caligari/The Cabinet of Dr Caligari* (Robert Wiene, 1920) or *Repulsion* (Roman Polanski, 1965), or explicitly marked flashbacks, hallucinations and dream sequences. Interpreting these coded images is part of what we learn when we learn to watch films.

The key point relating to *The Descent* is that films tend towards the exploration of subjective realities (and thus cohere around one or a handful of individuals), and that distinguishing between subjective and objective realities in film is difficult but generally possible through a kind of interpretive shorthand. *The Descent* takes a slightly different tack: here the subjective and objective realities can no longer be distinguished, Sarah's subjectivity is so fragmented and untrustworthy that the explicit revelation of her psychosis casts doubt on the stability of the entire enterprise.

Vision, the privileged mode of perception for modern mankind, proves unreliable throughout the film, a point struck forcefully home by repeated images of assaults on eyes: the pipe that in Sarah's dream penetrates her eye socket, the thumbs buried deep in a crawler's eyes, the tusk in an eye. Rebecca raises the point of the fallibility of vision early on in her discussion of the different kinds of hallucination the party may find themselves prone to, leading perhaps to their dismissal of Sarah's initial sighting of a crawler as a hallucination. In a sense they are right to distrust it: Sarah insists that 'I saw a man!', and thinks that he might be able to help them, although quite what help a naked hairless albino might offer two miles beneath the earth's surface is uncertain. Even seeing and accepting the existence of the crawlers hardly helps the cavers to survive.

The crawlers themselves are, of course, blind, but function perfectly well within the cave system – better, indeed, than the cavers themselves – and in the world outside, if we take their successful hunts as evidence. Finally Sarah's hallucinations are principally visual – that is, other sense data tend to fall into line with what she sees. Indistinguishable ultimately from any framing device, Sarah's hallucinations demonstrate the limits of vision: don't always believe what you see.

This inability to distinguish between subjective and objective realities suggests that subjectivity itself may be psychotic, or that psychosis is the logical end point, the limit case, of a certain stress on subjectivity. This might seem like a pointless consideration: surely narratives necessarily and inescapably revolve around selves? Cultural theorist Frederic Jameson, discussing in *The Political Unconscious* the tribal narratives explicated by anthropologist Claude Levi-Strauss, thinks not:

> These are evidently preindividualistic narratives; that is, they emerge from a social world in which the psychological subject has not yet been constituted as such, and therefore in which later categories of the subject, such as the 'character', are not relevant. Hence the bewildering fluidity of these narrative strings, in which human characters are ceaselessly transformed into animals or objects and back again; in which nothing like narrative 'point of view', let along 'identification' or 'empathy' with this or that protagonist, emerges. (1981: 124)

Jameson goes on to explain:

> the historical situation in which the emergence of the ego or centered subject can
> be understood: the dissolution of the older organic or hierarchical social groups, the
> universal commodification of the labor-power of individuals and their confrontation as
> equivalent units within the framework of the market, the *anomie* of these now 'free'
> and isolated individual subjects to which the protective development of a monadic
> armature alone comes as something of a compensation. (1981: 153-4)

Yet this 'centered subject' suffers from a certain limitation of consciousness that a
person in a preindividualistic society might not have experienced. In short, our modern
isolation means that we have no way of knowing whether what is happening to us is
real or not: our consciousness is delimited by our selves. This is what makes Sarah's
descent into madness acutely distressing: it reminds us of our own condition. The limits
of our knowledge can only ever be our own experience, not to be transcended except,
perhaps, through mysticism. *The Descent* suggests that we are trapped within ourselves,
with no real possibility of union or communication. Sarah's dilemma is, in a sense, at the
heart of what it means to be a modern human, demonstrating the limits, and perhaps
the fundamental untrustworthiness, of our particular brand of consciousness.

Having emerged, however, the 'centered subject' is here to stay; we cannot turn back the
clock and return to older organic social groups. Harking back to this state is futile; like
each individual's existence in the womb, it is a state impossible to return to, however
appealing the idea might be. In this respect we can understand Sarah's psychotic
subjectivity as expressing yet another form of archaic nostalgia: here for a time before
the emergence of the modern subject, another return to origins.

Perhaps, finally, Sarah goes mad because she is a woman – or, more precisely, that
the form her madness takes is explicitly feminine. Marshall draws here on an age-old
association of woman with madness, and a trend in classical cinema to allow women
subjectivity only to disallow it on the grounds that such subjectivity is demonstrably
untrustworthy, as in films such as *Possessed* (Curtis Bernhardt, 1947).

Of course, there are innumerable films about men going mad; some of these even
depict the male psychotic's interior experience, especially latterly in films like *Fight Club*

(David Fincher, 1999) and *The Machinist* (Brad Anderson, 2004). Yet representations of female madness seem to perform a function that is denied as a rule to their male counterparts; in them there is often no 'outside', no reliable exterior by which we can judge the trustworthiness of the interior experience. Female madness threatens to contaminate the narrative; it is uncontained, disrupting the very process of narrativity. While a detailed discussion of these issues is outside the scope of this book, we can outline some general trends.

In *The Descent* we know that Sarah has gone mad; we cannot know for certain when this madness begins, or what lies 'outside'. In *Images* (Robert Altman, 1972), the viewer experiences Cathryn's (Susannah York) struggle to distinguish interior from exterior experience, and is finally just as baffled as she is: hallucinations are routinely mistaken for 'reality', and vice versa. In *Rosemary's Baby* (Roman Polanski, 1968), the question of whether Rosemary (Mia Farrow) is paranoid or really has been impregnated with the devil's seed is never adequately answered; her final vision of the Satanists surrounding her baby's cot has, in keeping with the rest of the film, a hallucinatory quality that might mark it as expressive of a profound psychotic break. *Mulholland Dr.* (David Lynch, 2001) and *Inland Empire* (Lynch, 2006) go further still into their female characters' psychoses, collapsing any kind of reliable distinction between interior and exterior experience, subjective and objective, their diegeses contaminated beyond repair by madness. Even in films not explicitly concerned with madness, the dividing line between fantasy and reality is traditionally often more difficult to distinguish with female protagonists: think of *Persona* (Ingmar Bergman, 1966), *Belle de Jour* (Luis Buñuel, 1967), *Giulietta degli spiriti/ Juliet of the Spirits* (Federico Fellini, 1965), etc.

Compare representations of male madness. For a start there are classically very few films that represent it from an interior or subjective viewpoint – *The Cabinet of Dr Caligari* is a rare example, not only of male interiority but also a male madness that is uncontained and threatens to spill over into the bracketing narrative. The subjective madness explored in *Le locataire/The Tenant* (Roman Polanski, 1976) could be attributed to the fact that the eponymous tenant Trelkovsky (Polanski) believes that he is being turned into the previous tenant of his flat, a woman; yet even here we see flashes of 'objective' reality that delimit Trelkovsky's psychosis.

Representations of male madness have tended to focus more on exteriority, on actions; cue the psycho killers littering cinemas from M (Fritz Lang, 1931) onwards, or the sanity as madness trope of films like One Flew Over the Cuckoo's Nest (Milos Forman, 1975). A recent trend for exploring subjective male madness nearly always brackets the protagonists' experiences, making the films puzzles with well-defined answers: there is an 'outside', or containment, at work in films like The Machinist or Fight Club, along with a sense that these hallucinations are useful somehow, rational even in their attempts to tell their protagonists something. Finally, we know ultimately what's 'real' and what is a hallucination in these films.

There are, of course, films with male protagonists in which fantasy and reality are indistinguishable, but they tend not to revolve around issues of madness. In 8 _ (Federico Fellini, 1963), for instance, there is no suggestion that Guido Anselmi (Marcello Mastroianni) is losing his mind. The protagonists of Videodrome (David Cronenberg, 1983) and eXistenZ (Cronenberg, 1999) may be more confused by their constant reality slips, but these are films about technology rather than madness, a technology moreover implicitly figured as masculine – even if these protagonists are not in control, there is the suggestion that somebody else is. The same applies for a rash of films exploring male interiority as a kind of psychic theme park: The Cell (Tarsem Singh, 2000), Identity (James Mangold, 2003), The Jacket (John Maybury, 2005) and Inception (Christopher Nolan, 2010) are all buttressed by a sense of technological mastery in their techniques of burrowing into men's minds. It is generally only in representations of female madness that we are left entirely at sea, rudderless and adrift.

Given Clover's contention that cinematic identification crosses gender boundaries – that a male viewer can identify with a female character, and vice versa – we may well transfer her question about the victim's role in horror to this situation. What, then, is to be gained for a male viewer in running narratives of loss of cognitive control through a woman? The answer is twofold. Firstly and most obviously, we can take woman's long association with madness, itself related to an antique association between woman and the irrational, woman and nature; even women's bodies were classically conceived as betraying rationality, 'hysteria' famously thought to be caused by the wandering of the uterus around the body. Such associations informed the early language and practice of psychoanalysis, and remain with us today.

The second point depends on the first: if woman is irrational, untrustworthy, out of control, then man is perforce rational, trustworthy, masterful. Here we can rephrase Clover's question: what kind of repressed desires might be served for male viewers by running fantasies of uncontained madness through a female character? The answer might be precisely this loss of control, this abdication of mastery, of responsibility. Yet what could possibly be liberating about an experience that, in the films under discussion, is demonstrably traumatic? Rosemary Jackson offers a tentative answer in her conception of the subversive potential of the fantastic:

> it has been possible to claim for the fantastic a subversive function in attempting to depict a reversal of the subject's cultural formation. If the symbolic is seen as 'that unity of semantic and syntactic competence which allows communication and rationality to appear' (White, p.8), the imaginary area which is intimated in fantastic literature suggests all that is other, all that is absent from the symbolic, outside rational discourse. Fantasies of deconstructed, demolished or divided identities and of disintegrated bodies, oppose traditional categories of unitary selves. They attempt to give graphic depictions of subjects *in process*, suggesting possibilities of innumerable other selves, of different histories, different bodies. [...] This does not imply that subjects can exist outside of ideology and of the social formation, but that fantasies image the possibility of radical cultural transformation through attempting to dissolve or shatter the boundary lines between the imaginary and the symbolic. (1981: 177-178)

Sarah's identity may be deconstructed or divided, but this conveys a certain excitement for the viewer through its reminder that our own sense of coherence may be illusory. While the self strives to maintain its illusion of coherence, one of the appeals of *The Descent*, and indeed of horror films in general, is that it demonstrates the fragility of this coherence – through a wilful blurring of boundaries inside and outside, a breakdown of identity, or images of violated bodily integrity – in a controlled environment, as 'entertainment'. Horror can shed some light on our fractured and chaotic lives.

Fear is not disturbing because it intimates that the fabric of our lives, an apparently orderly weave, is being disrupted or is about to be disrupted, but because it shows us that the fabric has always been laddered and frayed. What is aberrant is not the disconcerting sensation of dread but rather the fantasies of order superimposed upon life to make it look seamless and safe (Cavallaro 2002: vii). Life, in *The Descent*, looks anything but seamless and safe; but the vertiginous dread induced by Sarah's madness conveys a giddying sensation we can enjoy as entertainment, safe in the knowledge that we can continue to ignore it as we go about our day-to-day lives.

FAMILY

Neil Marshall has in various interviews cited *Deliverance*, *Alien* and *The Shining* as the principal cinematic influences on *The Descent*, and the three offer a useful way to triangulate his film's co-ordinates. Marshall sets a high bar here – the three films are notable peaks in horror's back catalogue (even allowing for *Deliverance*'s shaky genre credentials) and it is to *The Descent*'s credit that it doesn't come off as insufferably cheap by comparison.

Before we consider the films' thematic and stylistic similarities, it's worth looking at their tone. All three have a weightiness unleavened by throwaway humour, a downbeat intensity and sense of darkness only made more effective by the compassion they show for their characters. Horror cinema might seem a strange place to look for compassion, but empathy for its characters is paramount for the genre to be truly effective. However entertaining it might be to watch grotesquely unlikeable US teens being sliced and diced by the latest psycho killer doing the rounds, such films can only ever be disposable, throwaway. A callous, cynical approach to horror characters is one of the more egregious qualities distinguishing most modern horror films (including the bulk of the 'Splat Pack' entries) from their forebears. By contrast *The Descent*, like its cited influences, shows not only care for its characters but also a sense that what we are seeing is worthwhile, that is means something.

Deliverance, *Alien* and *The Shining* are, like *The Descent*, about small groups isolated in hostile conditions with something unexpected and nasty. All three films play on fears of isolation and explore intra-group tensions alongside their more overt horror content; in *The Shining* the two are broadly indistinguishable. Beyond these thematic similarities, Marshall notes in 'The Making of *The Descent*' that each film relates to aspects of his in different ways: *Deliverance* is about an adventure trip that goes wrong, *Alien* is about atmosphere and menace and dark spaces, and *The Shining* is about someone going insane.

The similarities go further. *The Descent* shares *Deliverance*'s single-sex group of adventure tourists, raising corresponding questions about the politics of adventure and urbanoia's classic theme of city vs country. Both films acknowledge the allure of survivalism or a return to nature while reminding us that the shackles of civilisation have *something* going for them, even if it's only good dentistry. *Deliverance*'s status as a borderline horror film is matched by *The Descent*'s avoidance of horror tropes until a good forty minutes into the film, and both share a certain indeterminacy, a willingness to leave loose ends: in *Deliverance* the question of whether or not Drew is shot, and whether or not the mountain man killed by Ed is one of the rapists. *The Descent* even borrows some of *Deliverance*'s imagery – Juno's top looks like it's been filched from Lewis's wardrobe, and *The Descent* tips a nod to Lewis's compound fracture with another off-puttingly graphic snapped limb – while both films anthropomorphise their environments, as evidenced in Lewis's lament that 'We're gonna rape this whole goddamn landscape'.

Alien gives us the tough, resourceful character of Ellen Ripley (Sigourney Weaver), the template for all subsequent kickass heroines, including Juno. Ridley Scott's film is also explicitly concerned with motherhood, pregnancy and birth: the Nostromo's computer is called Mother and *Alien* makes much of the contrast between the antiseptic technological 'birth' of the crew at the start of the film and the shockingly messy birth of the alien from Kane's stomach later. *Alien* is full of dark tunnels lit by torches and often inhabited by something dripping menacingly; Dallas is trapped in an air shaft filled with lethal cervical hatches, a classic BPMII situation (see **Return to the Source**), while much of the film's horror comes from its implicit comparison between alien incubation and human pregnancy. *Alien* even features its own 'descent', as Kane abseils down into the vast alien egg depository, while Juno's discovery of the crawler bone yard quotes Kane's first view of the Space Jockey.

The Shining is less of an obvious touchstone, although *The Descent* borrows its opening aerial shots tracking a vehicle through the forest on its way to a Terrible Place, and Kubrick's film has a quintessential BPMII sequence when Wendy (Shelly Duvall) tries to squeeze through a bathroom window that's just a little too small for her, trapping her in a bathroom while her demented husband chops the door down with an axe.

Jack Torrance (Jack Nicholson) may go mad, but his madness takes a very different form from Sarah's in *The Descent*. There is an 'outside' (see **Nightmares in a Damaged Brain**) to Jack's hallucinations – when Wendy finds him in the bar, for instance, we are reassured that his vision of the bartender has been just that, a vision, while the hallucinations themselves are elsewhere clearly marked through their poor reality testing. We know that, in human terms at least, Jack, Wendy and Danny (Danny Lloyd) are alone in the Overlook. The ontological status of the hallucinations becomes more troubling later in the film, the less they are evidently interior expressions of Jack's psychosis. Danny sees things too, and ultimately so does Wendy. Halloran (Scatman Crothers), the cook, is being economical with the truth when he tells Danny that the visions he has – the titular Shining, a talent probably shared by Jack himself – are like pictures in a book. They aren't: they bite, as shown in Danny's strangulation (although the film leaves the possibility open that Jack is the culprit here) or, more tellingly, in whatever it is that releases Jack from the larder. Kubrick here allows the possibility, or rather the certitude, of the supernatural, a theme entirely absent from The Descent.

John Carpenter's The Thing is another clear influence. Like The Descent, it is a single-sex cabin fever bummer revolving around issues of trust and a birth anxiety manifested in its themes of incubation and assimilation, while David Julyan's score for The Descent is routinely accused of steering a little too close to Morricone's bass pulses for Carpenter's tale of Arctic alien invasion. Aliens (James Cameron, 1986) is also referenced in the sheer number of crawlers attacking the party, and the claustrophobic, frenzied nature of the fight scenes.

Less obvious as an influence is Touching the Void, a documentary revolving like The Descent around issues of trust, endurance, broken legs and the protocol of dealing with an injured companion. This tale of Simon Yates cutting his climbing buddy Joe Simpson's rope on an ill-fated climb of an Andean mountain allows its characters to explain the motivation behind not only their expedition but all-adventure tourism, including The Descent's caving. Yates talks about the sense of freedom in getting away from the 'clutter' of 'our world', and points out that there is 'not a lot of risk in our lives now. And to add a bit of risk takes you out of the humdrum. In that sense it makes you feel more alive'.

These aside, I have selected a couple of films that deserve a closer look as The Descent's antecedents, whether for their theme of evolutionary backsliding (Death Line) or their use of prehistoric subterranean cannibals (The Pit); later I'll look at the films that followed in The Descent's wake.

Death Line aka *Raw Meat*

Alex, an American in London, and his girlfriend Pat see an unconscious man at the foot of the stairs at Russell Square Tube station. Alex thinks he's drunk but Pat insists they go for help; when they return with a Tube guard the body has gone. The police take an interest because of a number of other disappearances at the station. When Tube workers are then attacked one recovered body shows human bite marks. Who's been eating people at Russell Square Tube?

It took an American to make the finest London horror film. Superbly cast, with Donald Pleasance in perhaps his greatest role as the tea-mad Inspector Calhoun, and a brief cameo from a towering Christopher Lee as an unscrupulous MI5 operative, *Death Line*'s premise is simple but effective, drawing on a near-century of London Underground folklore: what goes on at the disused stations? The return of the repressed here is, as so often, a guilty secret: in 1892 a tunnel collapsed, burying twelve Tube construction workers alive. The company building the line had gone bankrupt, and a rescue operation would have proved prohibitively costly, so the workers were abandoned to their fate. Rumours sprung up that they might have survived, at least temporarily, by resorting to cannibalism, but who would they turn to when they had nobody else left to eat?

The monster in *Death Line* is the Man, a descendant of the original trapped workers, who waylays stragglers on the Tube to feed not only himself but also his pregnant partner, who is dying, making him the last of his kind. A steady diet of late-night revellers and a complete absence of sunshine have done nothing for the Man's health: he has septicaemia, probably contracted from the rats that are his constant companions, acute vitamin deficiency and appalling skin, making *The Descent*'s crawlers look like models of health by comparison.

Life in the tunnels has led to a kind of evolutionary regression. The Man has the use of fire, as shown in his lanterns, a throwback in themselves, but his lair is strewn with straw, resembling a stable, and at one point he bites the head off a rat, marking him as on a par with a carny geek, barely human; he is also remarkably strong, and likes to hunt in the dark. He has lost the power of speech, except the time-hallowed Underground mantra 'Mind the doors!', which is for him a catch-all phrase, used tentatively as he attempts to seduce an abducted Pat then more loudly as his frustration with her resistance mounts.

For all the Man's homicidal, cannibalistic tendencies and unwholesome appearance, he is clearly a sympathetic figure. His parents – or perhaps grandparents, even – were abandoned to their deaths for economic reasons, leaving him and his kind to fend for themselves as best they can. He marks his partner's death with howls of grief, showing him to be in some ways a more humane character than some of his peers in the overground world: James Manfred OBE, for instance, is shown frequenting striptease parlours and offering a fellow Tube passenger money for sex, while the MI5 operative's mission seems to be to maintain Manfred's reputation – at any cost.

While the '70s stylings of Alex and Pat's apartment look entertainingly dated, the Man's lair has a timeless quality. The tunnels are dark and dank, dripping and dangerous, with a decidedly intrauterine quality, while the larger spaces he frequents look convincingly abandoned, littered with the ghostly detritus of a city whose dreams of progress blind it to the plight of anything left behind. The presence of the Man is almost incidental to the creepiness of these passages. At the end of the film there is a long take inside one of the dark, dripping tunnels, as the sounds of the police grow ever fainter; it is the place itself that is terrifying rather than its inhabitant, another womblike space threatening assimilation, reincorporation and an archaic return.

Creep

In 2004 Creep made a far more tiresome use of the underground setting, reprising Death Line's foreigner in London with Kate (Franka Potente), a German blonde who finds herself locked in the Underground overnight after an abortive attempt to get to a party. Kate, who seems until this point to have had nothing worse to worry about in her life than a broken heel, now has to deal with a coke-snorting rapist, smelly homeless people and a bald, screeching amateur doctor, whose appearance anticipates Marshall's crawlers. Winning our disdain from the off by waving large banknotes in front of the homeless characters in a bid to buy their obedience, Kate soon finds her world of pampered privilege receding into the distance as she is forced to trade in her heels for a pair of boots in order to navigate the train tracks, snaps off a fingernail and takes a tumble into a sewer.

Creep draws on *Subway* (Luc Besson, 1985) as much as horror tropes in its depiction of an Underground society, but proves more formulaic finally than any of its influences in its parade of stock characters: the aggressively coked-up banker, the homeless Scots junkie, the affable, disposable black buddy, the jobsworth security guard. Eventually the film lurches into medical horror, as Kate finds herself in the kind of grimy torture chamber that featured heavily in '00s horror, confused by hints of a backstory that never really delivers.

Perhaps *Creep*'s most egregious fault is that the empty Tube and its hidden backstage don't carry any kind of atmospheric kick: the Tube simply looks like the Tube, and the other spaces have a generic industrial feel, a wet Sunday in Storage King rather than the sub-*Eraserhead* atmosphere apparently attempted. We are left with the feeling that something vital is missing from the story, but without caring what it might be. Finally, *Creep*'s most notable achievement may be in its depiction of Kate as perhaps the least stereotyped German in British cinema.

The Pit

Pity poor Jamie (Sammy Snyders). Since his parents moved to the neighbourhood he has managed to alienate not only his classmates but also the local librarian, with whom he has an erotic obsession, and a series of babysitters, none of whom can tolerate his natural twelve-year-old's curiosity about their naked bodies for long. Jamie's only friends are the snakes and toads he keeps in his vivarium, and the teddy bear who eggs him on to ever wilder excesses in his war of attrition with the neighbours. But Jamie's luck changes when he finds a pit in the woods nearby inhabited by hairy man things. What on earth could they eat?

A guilty pleasure, *The Pit* boasts surprisingly high production values for such an aberrant tale, with a sun-soaked, all-American feel that makes it play like a peculiarly twisted episode of *The Brady Bunch*, an association helped by the casting of Snyders, fresh from playing Tom Sawyer in *Huckleberry Finn and His Friends* (TV, 1980), in the lead role.

Jamie is an unusual boy, but his enemies are such cretinous specimens that you can't help rooting for the oddball. One boy punches him in the face when Jamie tells him he'd like to join his gang; Abergail (Andrea Swartz), the girl next door, calls him 'clumsy stupid' and tricks him into trying to ride a partially disassembled bike; a wheelchair-bound old lady laments that he'll probably grow up to be 'one of those hippies'; and worst of all, his latest babysitter Sandra's boyfriend, a college sports champ, offers to teach him 'football'.

Needless to say they all meet their fate at the claws of the 'trollologs', as Jamie terms his furry friends, once he's established that candy bars don't impress them and that he can't keep on stealing money from Sandra (Sandy O'Reilly) to pay for meaty treats. To be fair, Jamie exhausts all other possibilities before luring the straights to the pit, trying to heft a side of beef from the back of a freezer lorry and tug a cow to its death, and he's careful, with one notable exception, to have only the bad people fed to the 'trollologs'. When this particular food source dries up he simply helps them to escape the pit ...

Sandra is alone in recognising the vertiginous implications of Jamie's discovery; Jamie doesn't want to tell anyone about them, as he fears they'll be kept in a cage, and the local authorities finally take them for a pack of wild dogs, wilfully blind to their upright gait. One of the locals apes Jamie's 'trollolog' misnomer by speculating that they might be 'those orange utan things', while Jamie's probably closer to the mark in telling Sandra that they're from 'prehistoric times'. Whatever the case, they look like shaggy Morlocks and have very sharp teeth, shown at work in a handful of gory flesh-rending sequences.

All of which begs the question: what kind of audience is the film 'pitted' at? *The Pit* is an upscale production using a leading child actor to front a tale that plays like outsider vengeance fantasy. There's a wrongness about the film that is occasionally genuinely shocking: Jamie's prurient interest in his babysitter and librarian sit uncomfortably in today's less playful times, and the gore of later scenes seems at odds with the jaunty jokiness of Jamie's initial attempts to feed the 'trollologs'. Whatever its makers intended, it seems to have been a career crusher for Snyders, perhaps over-keen to shake off his innocent image. But if the modern viewer can sit through its sillier excesses it has a certain twisted charm.

* * *

After *The Descent*, the deluge. The success of Marshall's film meant that the cave was once more a bankable Terrible Place, even if for most of the films that followed it was little more than somewhere to hide your monster, as in *Alone in the Dark* (Uwe Boll) and *It Waits* (Stephen R. Monroe, both 2005). Timewasters like *Caved In: Prehistoric Terror* spend more time in their caverns, but pull up short, in spite of their gory effects, of being true horror films. The same goes for *The Cave*, pipped by a month to a theatrical release in the UK by *The Descent*, although fellow bandwagon-hopper *The Cavern* at least attempts a more straightforwardly scary approach.

Themes from *The Descent* are perhaps more fruitfully explored in a rash of feature films and documentaries following Marshall's trajectory of wilderness adventure gone wrong. *Grizzly Man* (Werner Herzog) was released in the same year as *The Descent*, and Herzog's documentary shares some qualities with Marshall's film: Timothy Treadwell has rejected civilisation (save for some of its trappings – a DV camera and the helicopter rides that drop him off in Alaskan bear country) in favour of a return to nature. Yet his idea of nature is an illusion, a construct that reveals more about him than about his environment. Herzog rejects not only Treadwell's valorisation of nature – for the director 'the common denominator of the universe is not harmony but chaos, hostility and murder' – but also his sense of kinship with the bears: 'what haunts me is that in all the faces of all the bears that Treadwell ever filmed, I discover no kinship, no understanding, no mercy. I see only the overwhelming indifference of nature. To me, there is no such thing as a secret world of the bears. And this blank stare speaks only of a half-bored interest in food.'

Into the Wild (Sean Penn, 2007), a feature film based on another true story of a wilderness adventure gone wrong, features a protagonist (Chris McCandless, played by Emile Hirsch) whose rejection of civilisation goes further still. He donates his college funds to Greenpeace, burns most of his possessions and remaining money and heads for Alaska, where his pastoral dream is cut rudely short by poor seasonal planning and a foraging mishap. Similar films 'based on a true story', such as *127 Hours* (Danny Boyle, 2010) and *The Way Back* (Peter Weir, 2010), soon followed.

This trend of what we might call endurance cinema seems to have filled a gap previously reserved in film for the Western. That more pastoral mode for the relationship between man and landscape has effectively vanished or become untenable, even as pastiche. Endurance cinema takes its cues from other cultural developments: obviously adventure tourism and extreme sports, but also a kind of pessimistic anti-Romanticism, or a nostalgia for something lost, or recoverable only at great cost. The characters' quests in these films is for authenticity in a reified world; for a sense of the sacred, even, in a world that offers only the blandness of mediated religion. It is telling in this respect that both *Grizzly Man* and *Touching the Void*, perhaps the key film in this trend, describe their characters' experiences in quasi-mystical terms: Treadwell wants to become a bear, while Joe Simpson speaks of becoming 'almost nothing', of melting into the landscape.

One point arising from these films that seems particularly pertinent for *The Descent*, and indeed for all of Neil Marshall's films, is that we only live through co-operation. Whatever near-religious impulse may drive us to a solitary engagement with the wilderness, ultimately we need each other to survive. McCandless in *Into the Wild* turns his back on offers of human companionship and dies as a result; *The Way Back* is all about the sacrifices individuals must make for the good of the group.

A point less obviously raised by these films, but applying to them all (with the exception of *The Way Back*) is that this 'return to nature' or retreat from the comforts of civilisation is a choice available only to those who enjoy such comforts in the first place. The idea of hiking for pleasure would be anathema to, say, a Guatemalan villager who has to walk several miles daily simply to fetch water or firewood. Once again, the idea of nature as a valuable good is only available to those who are irreparably severed from it; adventure tourism represents the self-indulgence of the leisure classes who have money to burn, a point that may allow us to empathise with these characters as we watch them in comfortable cinemas or on our home DVD systems, but should remind us that the response of most of the rest of the world may be closer to that of Treadwell's bears, a 'blank stare [that] speaks only of a half-bored interest in food'.

The politics of adventure aside, the following films have been selected for more in-depth analysis: *The Cave*, for its overt narrative similarities with *The Descent*; *The Cavern*, for its engagingly tweaked riff on cave iconography; *The Descent: Part 2* (Jon Harris, 2009) for obvious reasons; and *Sanctum* (Alister Grier, 2011), for running *The Descent*'s mixture of extreme sports and birth imagery through a father-son relationship.

The Cave

Dr Nicolai (Marcel Iures) hires a crack team of cave divers led by Jack McAllister (Cole Hauser) to help him explore a virgin cave system in the Carpathian Mountains. They soon find they're not alone in the caves: someone has been there before them, and now they are under attack. When their exit is blocked by a rock fall, they have no option but to go deeper into the cave.

On the surface there are enough similarities between *The Descent* and *The Cave* to understand Lionsgate's delay in releasing Marshall's film in the US. Another group of cavers becomes trapped inside an unexplored system where they are attacked by echolocating, toothy predators. Again there are tensions within the group, revolving around sexual competition (Jack and his brother Tyler [Eddie Cibrian] vie for the attentions of biologist Kathryn [Lena Headey]); again a monster is subjected to the kind of cod-scientific examination that has been mandatory since 50s American horror films; and again a couple of nasty leg injuries slow the group down.

But the similarities are never more than cosmetic. Where *The Descent* is a dynamic film, wringing the maximum from every situation, not only in terms of tension but also in its symbolic richness, *The Cave* remains flat and inert, refusing to make anything more substantial out of its subject matter. *The Cave* is moreover less a horror film than an adventure film whose monsters lend it a little extra spice. Its characters comprise a professional team, rather than *The Descent*'s group of weekend sports enthusiasts, and one made up of pretty women and unlikeably square-jawed men given to macho posturing and ludicrously bombastic dialogue. In tone this leaves it closer to *Team America Go Scuba*, a point reinforced by the unfortunate resemblance between the team's first base at Titan Hall and *Thunderbirds*'Tracy Island.

In the light of *The Descent*, it's notable how little use *The Cave* makes of its setting: apart from the antique myths of winged demons we learn have been told about the cave, the film fails to mobilise any of its environment's rich symbolic associations. Here the system is simply an unexplored dark space where nasty things can happen. The idea of naming new caves is raised – the team is told, 'You find it, you name it', and Kathryn says that 'Whenever I find something unique, I want to put my name on it' – but the lead is never followed up, making this just one of a string of evacuated ideas paid no more than lip service in the film.

Against *The Descent*'s atavism we have a techno fetishism manifesting itself in meaningless babble about the group's kit, lavish attention paid to their advanced comms equipment and an overuse of unconvincing CGI throughout. Some of the plot points are astonishingly witless: nobody seems very surprised to find they are sharing a cave system with winged monsters, although the cave's ecosystem appears until their arrival to have been all predators and no prey; and everyone unquestioningly accepts Kathryn's 'scientific' explanation for the monsters, as previous cavers who have been radically mutated by a ubiquitous parasite.

The cave network itself, with its succession of large spaces and lack of constricted tunnels, looks about as realistic as the subterranean world of *Journey to the Center of the Earth* (Henry Levin, 1959), and is lit accordingly, while the cavers respond to it in increasingly credibility-straining ways until finally they are wandering around ice caves in wet T-shirts without a hint of discomfort.

The Cavern

Five American cavers, two Kazakh guides and a writer are the first to explore a cave system in a remote, uncharted part of Kazakhstan. For Gannon (Mustafa Shakir), the team leader, the expedition is an opportunity to lay a ghost to rest: two years ago he lost his fiancee during a flood in a Peruvian cave. When Slava (Neno Pervan), their cave guide, is disembowelled shortly after their descent into the cave, they realise there is something else in the cave with them. Their exit is blocked and their rope back to the top severed – is there any other way out?

The Cavern follows *The Descent*'s formula fairly slavishly: the grief/guilt nexus at the heart of the story, the leadership tussles and intra-group tensions, the lure of the unexplored system, the ethics of abandoning an injured companion – even the UK DVD jacket design is a dead ringer for *The Descent*'s US release art – but is saddled with a screenplay so risible it was never going to steal Marshall's thunder.

After the team – financed, improbably, by taking photos inside unexplored cave systems, remarkably one of *The Cavern*'s less unbelievable plot points – drives in two jeeps to the cave area, we learn that 'This area hasn't been mapped yet, it's officially unexplored'. It takes some chutzpah, or a gleeful idiocy, to throw out information like this in a time of GPS and Google Earth, when we've just seen the team drive along tracks to their destination. The dialogue gets even fruitier when Domingo (Andres Hudson), a Hispanic 'brujo', starts making portentous comments about caving: 'There's something about caves that's alive, there's something down here that – if we're open to it, we can connect with. I look for that connection every time I go down ... I crave it.' When the shit hits the fan in the cave Domingo's response is to chant and intone gnomically, 'None of this is explainable in physical means'. Even this is pipped, however, by Slava's wild lines immediately before vanishing: 'The cave is moaning. It is making love. It is fucking you!'

Domingo's shamanic gibberish gives a whiff of the supernatural absent from Marshall's film, although *The Cavern* eventually pulls back for a wholly materialist explanation of events. Domingo, perhaps craving communion with 'cave spirits', 'the most unpredictable of all', refuses to run when the group is attacked, unfortunately losing the film its most engaging character. His runner-up in the watchability stakes, the adenoidally nerdy writer Ambrose (Danny Jacobs), whose freakouts in the cave provide perhaps the film's most entertaining scenes, soon follows, leaving us with the kind of bland professionals we last saw trapped in *The Cave*. The end comes after a mercifully brief 76 minutes, but even that is too long to be exposed to the female characters' perpetual whining of 'omigodomigod' without reaching for the fwd button – if *The Descent*'s representation of women gave you pause for thought, you'll probably want to give *The Cavern* a wide berth.

For all that there's something appealing about the film. Apart from the ripe dialogue and a general air of ineptitude shading into genuine weirdness, the look of the film is peculiar enough to make even jaded viewers pay attention. One of *The Cavern*'s stranger visual gambits is to look like a *Blair Witch*-style vérité film when there's no camera written into the diegesis; so we have all the artefacts of video recording – the shaky camera, poor image quality, throwaway framing, etc. – with no diegetic rationale to back it up. The opening exterior scenes are inexplicably shot with a sepia tint so strong they look like the beginning of *Bagpuss*, while *The Cavern* follows *The Descent*'s disorienting technique of having the cave lit only by the cavers' torches, and adds dry ice for a fuzzed-out effect that makes it even harder to see what's going on. The attacks push this visual incomprehensibility into overdrive, comprising whirls of flashing lights and rapid edits that fail to provide any comprehensible information and look finally completely abstract, like Stan Brakhage films. Elsewhere the image is occasionally and arbitrarily flipped, so the characters appear to be crawling along the cave ceiling or drilling into the cave wall upside down. Presumably these are attempts to convey the disorientation felt by the cavers, but the effect is more distancing than intended, inviting the viewer to enjoy the strobing lights and flashes of colour as pure abstract visual pleasure.

The Descent: Part 2

A rescue team comes to the end of their second day looking for the women at Boreham Caverns when a bloodied and amnesiac Sarah stops a car some distance away. Sheriff Lynch (Josh Cole) is notified and uses tracker dogs to establish that she emerged from Chapel Mine, a disused mine working. The sheriff suspects Sarah of having killed her companions, and insists on taking her, along with Deputy Rios (Krysten Cummings), a female cop, and three members of the rescue team, into the cave network at Chapel Mine. Cue crawler attacks.

The Descent was never going to be an easy film to follow, not least because Marshall wrote his screenplay without a sequel in mind. It has been noted that Marshall's film plays like two films in itself – *Alien* and *Aliens* – ramping up the terror of its first half with an explosion of frenzied violence in the second. Given that Marshall's film ends with an excess of savagery that is difficult to top, it leaves the sequel with nowhere to go. Director Harris (*The Descent*'s editor) and his three scriptwriters attempt to solve this problem by simply providing more of the same, resolving some issues left open at the end of the first film and seizing on any opportunity Marshall leaves for grossing out an audience even more.

More of the same: *The Descent: Part 2* quotes Marshall's film so clearly and so often that the viewer inevitably wishes they were watching the original. The typeface and retro lens flare from Marshall's film are present and correct, along with the music, while the film again opens with aerial shots of the Appalachian mountains. Sarah sees a crawler early on in the cave system, which is discounted as a hallucination; the team discover Holly's DV camera in the boneyard, and run through what look like outtakes from *The Descent* on it until they see the original reveal of the crawlers, which prompts its own crawler attack this time around. Sam's wristwatch scene is quoted when one of the rescue team's walkie-talkies explodes into life while she is hunted by a crawler; and the film ends with an escape from the cave system that directly quotes Sarah's 'escape' in *The Descent*.

Resolution: Sarah's psychosis has conveniently receded into amnesia – she can't remember what happened to her friends. This has the happy consequence of allowing the film to slot neatly onto both the US and UK endings of the film. The whiskery old-timer who finds Sarah reveals more about previous visitors to the cave system: his grandfather had gone missing exploring it – 'Folks reckon he must have broken clean through into hell' – providing an explanation for the piton and helmet found during the first film. We also learn more about *The Descent*'s cavers: Juno is one Senator Kaplan's daughter, which is the main reason Lynch has a wild hair up his ass about finding her presumed killer. But Juno is still alive, killing crawlers in the dark. This gives Juno and Sarah the chance to kiss and make up, and Sarah the opportunity to redeem her selfish behaviour at the end of the first film with an act of self-sacrifice. The bodies of Rebecca and Sam are found in situ, slasher-style, and only marginally gnawed; for large predators the crawlers evidently leave a lot of meat on their prey.

Gross out: *The Descent: Part 2* answers the pressing question of crawler sanitation and sewage by showing a crawler defecating into a pool, which Sarah and Rita subsequently fall into it in an attempt to top Marshall's pool of blood. That the scene doesn't really work is an indication that more than lip service needs to be paid to abjection to shock an audience; here as elsewhere, the symbolic content of the film seems to be empty or inert. But the film does succeed in being satisfyingly violent – one crawler takes a drill in the head, another has his skull crushed by a boulder, and the sheriff's wrist is macerated repeatedly with a pick – and the improbably adequate lighting of the sequel means its gore effects are highly visible.

The lighting elsewhere is a problem. While the film initially looks like it will copy Marshall and use only natural, or natural seeming, lighting (the cavers' torches, flares, etc.) it soon abandons this gambit, making the caves look like what they are: plastic tunnels. They are also, providing a graphic illustration of the lack of inspiration in the film, predominantly dry, missing the heavily lubricated intrauterine slickness of some of The Descent's tunnels. And while there are a couple of tight squeezes, in the main these are caves that can be run around, a narrative convenience insofar as the cops aren't trained climbers, but also a credibility-draining point, and a missed trick with regard to the film's atmosphere.

The film is at its best when it deviates from Marshall's model. The sheriff, shooting at a crawler, prompts a cave-in that traps Cath (Anna Skellern) in an isolated spot. Dan (Douglas Hodge), the leader of the rescue party, is unable to free her, leading to the nightmarish situation of Cath putting a brave face on being abandoned by the others as they move out of radio contact, and making for one of the few moments of genuine empathy in the film. Cath ends up being attacked in her cramped space, effectively combining claustrophobic isolation with violence in a way that The Descent never essays.

Predictably the film apes Marshall's bummer ending, though here the conclusion is difficult to unpack. It seems to be suggested by not only his actions at the end but also his wink at Rios as the team descends into the mine that the old man who discovers Sarah at the start is some kind of guardian or gatekeeper for Chapel Mine, responsible for keeping the cave system secret. The reason he doesn't just kill Sarah when he finds her initially is presumably because she is amnesiac and doesn't tell him where she's been. When he drags a stunned Rios back to the hole she crawled from, he seems on the verge of tipping her back in, not only to dispose of the body but also perhaps to feed the crawlers. His motivation – on first viewing the film it seems completely nonsensical – is obscure. If he is trying to keep the cave system secret, is that to protect the crawlers or prospective visitors? Surely as far as he is aware the sheriff has had to file a 'flight plan' of his own, meaning the location of their disappearance will be noted.

If his main intention is instead to provide the crawlers with food, why bother, given that they seem to be doing fine with the elk they drag down? Perhaps, finally, his motivation is simply that of a fictional character designed to provide a downbeat ending, and we'll leave it at that.

Sanctum

Papua New Guinea, the present. Esa Ela is the largest unexplored cave system in the world. Rich playboy Carl (Ioan Gruffudd) is funding a team headed by Frank McGuire (Richard Roxburgh) in a bid to find a route through from the cave entrance to the sea. But a storm is heading their way, and threatens to flood the cave; will they be able to get out before it's too late?

Sanctum is by no stretch a horror film, but its concerns dovetail in many ways more neatly with *The Descent* than do those of countless cave horror films – *The Boogens*, *Alien Terror*, etc. – with its themes of extreme sports, trust, the protocol of dealing with injured colleagues and womb/birth imagery.

Sanctum comes with a 'James Cameron presents' tag, and clearly hopes to piggyback on the success of *Avatar* (James Cameron, 2009) by recycling some of its tropes and themes: awe at the beauty of the natural world, conveyed through a highly artificial digital technology; a search for the sacred in a secular world, and a strong suspicion that it resides somewhere exotic; and a soundtrack to match, with enough generic ethnographic stylings to feel like an Enigma album on repeat play.

While *Avatar* pays at least lip service to some grander ideas – exploitation of indigenous peoples, environmental degradation – *Sanctum*'s concerns are entirely local, and quickly devolve onto the relationship between Frank and his son Josh (Rhys Wakefield). At the beginning of the film they are at loggerheads, with Josh blaming his father for the death of one of their party; by the end the father is teaching the son 'Kubla Khan' and allowing him to lead them out of the system. It's Frank and Josh's show: the other characters are only useful insofar as they hinder or help the father-son relationship, and are therefore entirely dispensable, killed off in sequence according to their importance to this narrative, with alternative father figure Carl correspondingly hanging around the longest.

One of the more curious aspects of *Sanctum* is its insistence on this being *the* key relationship, explored in a cave system that is inescapably coded as female and maternal. The group becomes trapped in the cave when the storm hits, and rising water levels force them to seek a way out through the 'devil's restriction'. This dangerously narrow passage leads finally to the open sea through a trial by ordeal that involves fights, violent deaths and mercy killings. This is a narrative of birth that refuses any consideration of the maternal; Josh's absent, presumably dead mother barely gets a mention. The principal function of the women here is less to nurture than to panic, to become hysterical, so hyper-feminine in their expression of emotion that Frank and Josh can display warmth towards each other without coming across as feminine.

Sanctum's caves look marginally more convincing than those in *The Cave*, but still not as credible as *The Descent*, despite the gross disparity between the films' budgets. Its beautifully shot underwater scenes make it fairly easy on the eye, but *Sanctum*'s principal point of interest is in its skewed gender politics, its vision of a technologically enhanced world of homosocial bonds in which women only count because they allow men to cry.

CONCLUSION

On the face of it, *The Descent* isn't *quite* up to the standard of the horror classics it seeks to emulate. This is hardly surprising, given that *Deliverance*, *The Shining*, *Alien* and *The Thing* are widely acknowledged as high points in the horror canon. Arguably the overly frenetic fight scenes and the uneven tone keep *The Descent* from being a true horror classic. So why should we pay it so much attention?

The Descent is interesting historically as one of the most critically and commercially successful releases in the recent British horror boom that also unleashed such dark, scary and mature works as *Eden Lake* (James Watkins, 2008), *The Children* (Tom Shankland, 2008) and *Kill List* (Ben Wheatley, 2011). And this return of an adult sensibility to horror was hardly confined to the UK. Even if major US studios continued to churn out uninspired 'reimaginings' of horror classics for the Facebook generation, some recent studio products have betrayed a sophistication at odds with the snarky knowingness of their '90s forebears. *Drag Me to Hell* (Sam Raimi, 2009) and *The Cabin in the Woods* (Drew Goddard, 2011) may be tongue-in-cheek and self-referential but they are also made with a gleeful intelligence and a respect for their audience that horror fans have long since learned never to take for granted. The same goes for US independents: today even an '80s retro horror film (*The House of the Devil* [Ti West, 2009]) can be made that trades in the irritating in-jokes and witless teens of the *Scream* saga for genuine terror, in a manner barely imaginable in the '90s.

Internationally the picture looks even more interesting, with glossy arthouse/horror crossover hits like *El laberinto del fauno/Pan's Labyrinth* (Guillermo del Toro, 2006) and *Låt Den Rätte Komma In/Let the Right One In* (Tomas Alfredson, 2008), displaying a bite that belied their crossover success, while hardcore horror fans were catered for by the dread weight of films like the French *Martyrs* (Pascal Laugier, 2008) and the South Korean *Akmareul boatda/I Saw the Devil* (Jee-woon Kim, 2010). These films' commitment to exploring an unremittingly bleak cinematic vision couldn't be further from the throwaway shock tactics of films like *Hostel* and *The Human Centipede* (Tom Six, 2009).

As for the 'splat pack', none except perhaps Marshall has lived up to their initial promise, and even Marshall stumbled badly with *Doomsday*. *The Saw* cycle continued to appeal to people too young to watch the films legally, a moot concern in our internet-enhanced days; *Haute Tension/Switchblade Romance*'s Alexandre Aja took the money and ran with some entertainingly trashy but eminently disposable remakes (*The Hills Have Eyes* in 2006, *Piranha* in 2010), a path also trodden by Rob Zombie (*Halloween* in 2007, *Halloween II* in 2009). Greg McLean disappointed with *Rogue* (2007), his 'giant croc' follow-up to the impressively downbeat *Wolf Creek* (2005); and Eli Roth has moved away from direction and further into film production since *Hostel II* (2007).

Obviously *The Descent* isn't solely responsible for the return of a mature, adult tone to horror in the mid-2000s; but it offers a marker for this shift; and a commercially highly successful one to boot. This is largely due to its effectiveness, and its effectiveness is due to – what, exactly? Viewers are near-unanimous in describing the scene in which the cavers squeeze through tight passages as the most tense, the most effective in the film. Marshall designed these scenes to play on viewers' claustrophobia, but the near-universality of their effectiveness suggests another reading, one that aligns itself with the intrauterine imagery running through the film.

By this reading the effectiveness of these scenes supports Otto Rank's contention that the trauma of birth is the originary human trauma, while the ease with which Stanislav Grof's mapping of the psychic analogues of the birth process can be locked on to the film suggests that *The Descent* is rich territory for exploring Rank and Grof's ideas.

It is here that Marshall's film becomes most interesting, most valuable. The womb and birth imagery of the film is so clearly evident that we can consider *The Descent* a manifest display of what may be latent in other films, to borrow the terms from psychoanalysis. A provisional acceptance of Rank and Grof's ideas affects the way we understand not only the content of horror (and, perhaps, its form) but also our interest in exposing ourselves to it, and offers a new understanding of certain horror themes and images at odds with the critical orthodoxy. While these issues deserve fully fleshed research of their own, this study of *The Descent* may act as a springboard to further research, for which space here permits a sketch only of the most basic ideas.

Take for example the standard academic reading of the horror trope of attempts to create life without birth – the many *Frankenstein* films, *Altered States* (Ken Russell, 1980), the two versions of *The Fly* (Kurt Neumann, 1958; David Cronenberg, 1986). Barbara Creed, an influential theorist, encapsulates an orthodox feminist reading with statements such as 'patriarchal ideology represents women's reproductive functions as abject in order to produce her as monstrous' (2005: 16). According to this reading the concept of creating life without birth represents attempts by man to usurp the reproductive powers of woman by replacing the uncanny, unseen womb with visible, measurable and rational science. Rank's idea introduces a complementary reading: what if these attempts by male scientists to wrest control of reproduction from women's wombs were finally more about creating life without the trauma of birth?

The centrality of the trauma of birth, and Grof's explication of it, also helps to explain the creepiness of the Terrible Places of horror, and the specific horror of the intrauterine passages of *Alien*, with its deadly cervical hatches, and the 'no exit' scenes from films like *The Shining*, in which Shelley Duvall, in an extremely tense bid to escape her husband's axe, tries to squeeze through a window opening that may prove a little too small for her.

Rank's ideas may also shed some light on why we should watch films like *The Descent* at all – why put ourselves through such gruelling experiences? Trauma, for Rank, necessarily recalls the birth trauma; repetition of the birth trauma, whether through analysis or art, can help to release, or abreact, the repressed emotions associated with it. What constitutes trauma first time around can be repeated as play; play that seeks to control and manage the original trauma. For Rank this repetition has a compulsive quality: we are compelled to repeat the birth trauma in order to abreact its effects.

This idea may help to explain Sarah's motivation in going on the caving expedition. Loss of a loved one may, for Rank, be particularly reminiscent of the primal trauma:

> When one loses a closely connected person of either sex, this loss reminds one again of the primal separation from the mother; and the painful task of disengaging the libido from this person ... corresponds to the psychical repetition of the primal trauma. In the different human customs of mourning it is undoubtedly clear ... that the mourner tries to identify himself with the dead, showing how he envies him the return to the mother. (2010: 35)

For Sarah, then, the trauma of her loss may inspire a 'phantasy' of reliving the birth trauma; this phantasy may, however, have at least the potential of helping to heal her. Carol Clover sees the urge to repeat something, 'to revisit, over and over again, an originary story in the hopes of getting it right' (1995: 176), as key to our enjoyment of horror:

> it is surely fair to say that horror is probably the most convention-bound of all popular genres, that its conventions are organized around the experience of fear, and that this conjunction – scary stories endlessly repeated – stands as a narrative manifestation of the syndrome of repetition compulsion (*Wiederholungszwang*)… The function and effects of repetition compulsion are not clear. (It is conspicuously driven, however, by the wish to 'get it right,' one of the oft-noted dynamics of horror films.) What is clear is that where there is *Wiederholungszwang* there is historical suffering – suffering that has been more or less sexualised as 'erotogenic masochism' …

> It is in the nature of repetition compulsion that the repeater 'does not recall [the] prototype' of the repetition scenario; 'on the contrary, he has the strong impression that the situation is fully determined by the circumstances of the moment'. (1995: 212-3)

For Rank both the 'function and effects of repetition compulsion' *are* clear: it serves to abreact the anxiety caused by the primal trauma, the 'historical suffering' whose origin we do not recall. Trauma, as we have seen, can be revisited and, this time, controlled, through art. The compulsion relies on an ambivalent attitude to control: for horror to be effective it must be immediate and convincing, and hold us in its thrall; film is a peculiarly effective medium because it imposes its own pace on the viewer. Yet we remain, ultimately, in control of the experience: trauma has been transmuted into play. We can leave the cinema, or cover our eyes; we can pause the DVD, even stop it altogether if the experience proves too much.

While other films explore the trauma of birth through scenes of incubation, hosting and pregnancy gone wrong, perhaps most notably in supernatural horror films like *The Entity* (Sidney J. Furie, 1982) and the *Alien* cycle, *The Descent* takes as its central motif a far more universal theme, that of the trauma of *being born*. That it is near-unique in doing so suggests that Rank's stress on the repression of this originary trauma is correct; the peculiar charge packed by the claustrophobic tunnel sequences and the explosive energy that floods the film once they have been left behind only support Rank's theories further.

And all this for a film that never explicitly mentions birth at all. Theoretical considerations aside, we owe Neil Marshall and his team a tip of the hard hat for creating one of the most viscerally effective horror films of recent years. And if you ever find yourself straying down a dark tunnel and wondering what's inside, just remember: take a higher path. Stick to the flight plan. And don't leave your medication behind.

BIBLIOGRAPHY

Bernard, M. (2010) 'Selling the Splat Pack: The DVD Revolution and the American Horror Film', unpublished PhD thesis

Cale, M. (2006) 'The Descent' in *Ruthless Reviews*, http://www.ruthlessreviews.com/1096/descent-the/

Campos, E. (2006) 'Neil Marshall begins our "Descent"' in *Film Threat*, http://www.filmthreat.com/interviews/1056/

Cavallaro, D. (2002) *The Gothic Vision*, London/New York: Continuum

Clover, C. (1992) *Men, Women and Chainsaws*, London: BFI

Creed, B. (1993) *The Monstrous-Feminine*, London: Routledge

Creed, B. (2005) *Phallic Panic*, Victoria: Melbourne University Press

Doane, M. (1987) *The Desire to Desire*, Bloomington: Indiana University Press

Edelman, D. (2006) 'Now Playing at Your Local Multiplex: Torture Porn' in *New York Magazine*

Eliade, M. (1964) *Myth and Reality*, London: Allen & Unwin

Freud, S. (1955) 'The "Uncanny"' in *The Complete Psychological Works of Sigmund Freud volume XVII*, Standard Edition, tr. James Strachey, London: Hogarth Press Ltd

Freud, S. (1959) *The Complete Psychological Works of Sigmund Freud volume XX*, Standard Edition, tr. James Strachey, London: Hogarth Press Ltd

Gonzalez, E. (2006) 'The Descent' in *Slant Magazine*, http://www.slantmagazine.com/film/review/the-descent/2145

Guillen, M. (2006) 'The Descent – Interview with Neil Marshall' in *Twitch Film*, http://twitchfilm.com/interviews/2006/07/the-descentinterview-with-neil-marshall.php

Jackson, R. (1981) *Fantasy*, London: Methuen

Jameson, F. (1981) *The Political Unconscious*, London: Methuen

Jones, A. (2006) 'The New Blood' in *Total Film*, April issue pp.100-106

Jung, C. (1986) *Four Archetypes*, London: Routledge

Lewis-Williams, D. (2002) *The Mind in the Cave*, London: Thames & Hudson

Morton, L. (2005) 'Mike and Lisa's Throwdown Review: The Descent' in *Chiaroscuro – Treatments of Light and Shade in Words*, http://www.chizine.com/throwdown_descent.htm

Nelson, V. (2001) *The Secret Life of Puppets*, Cambridge, Mass: Harvard University Press

Pike, D. (2009) 'Hiding in Plain Sight: Cinematic Undergrounds' in Jansson and Lagerkvist (eds) *Strange Spaces* pp.317-333, Farnham, Surrey: Ashgate

Rank, O. (2010) *The Trauma of Birth*, Connecticut: Martino Publishing

'ScoreKeeper' (2006) 'ScoreKeeper Chats With Composer David Julyan (MEMENTO, THE PRESTIGE)!!' in *Ain't it Cool News*, http://www.aintitcool.com/node/31031

Stax (2006) 'Comic-Con 2006: Neil Marshall Interview' in *IGN movies*, http://uk.movies.ign.com/articles/721/721301p1.html

Valdez, J. (2008) 'The Descent (2005)' in *This Distracted Globe*, http://thisdistractedglobe.com/2008/06/20/the-descent-2005/

Weinberg, F. (1986) *The Cave – The Evolution of a Metaphoric Field from Homer to Ariosto*, New York: Peter Lang

Beyond Hammer

British Horror Cinema Since 1970

James Rose

Devil's Advocates

"Auteur Publishing's new Devil's Advocates critiques on individual titles offer bracingly fresh perspectives from passionate writers. The series will perfectly complement the BFI archive volumes." Christopher Fowler, Independent on Sunday

Let the Right One In — Anne Billson

"Anne Billson offers an accessible, lively but thoughtful take on the '80s-set Swedish vampire belter... a fun, stimulating exploration of a modern masterpiece." Empire

Witchfinder General — Ian Cooper

"I enjoyed it very much; it sets out all the various influences, both before and after the film, and indeed the essence of the film itself, very well indeed." Jonathan Rigby, author of English Gothic

Saw — Benjamin Poole

"This is a great addition to a series of books that are starting to become compulsory for horror fans. It will also help you to appreciate just what an original and amazing experience the original SAW truly was." The Dark Side

The Texas Chain Saw Massacre — James Rose

"[James Rose] find[s] new and unusual perspectives with which to address [the] censor-baiting material. Unsurprisingly, the effect... is to send the reader back to the films... watch the films, read these Devil's Advocate analyses of them." Crime Time